252
Nichols

Copy 1

Storytelling the gospel

Storytelling the Gospel

C. William Nichols

Chalice  **Press**

St. Louis, Missouri

Cover: Michael Domínguez and Ed Koehler
Interior design: Lynne Condellone

This book is printed on acid-free, recycled paper.

Visit Chalice Press on the World Wide Web at
www.chalicepress.com

252
N

10 9 8 7 6 5 4 3 2 1   99 00 01 02 03 04

Library of Congress Cataloging–in–Publication Data

Nichols, William C.
    Storytelling the Gospel / by C. William Nichols.
        p.   cm.
    ISBN 0-8272-3438-4
    1. Story sermons.   2. Sermons, American.   I. Title.
BV4307.S7N53 1999
252– dc21   99-21211
                                                                  CIP

Printed in the United States of America

For
David and Claudia

—beloved son, cherished daughter—
whose persistent entreaties to
"tell me a story"
introduced me to the wonderful world of
storytelling

Contents

Foreword

Someone once said that communication is the most fragile of endeavors. You measure success by reducing the number of failures. And in this day of TV-induced ten-minute attention spans, and entertainment being what Neal Gabler calls the primary value of American culture, being able to tell a good story is a must to reach people.

That's just as true for preaching the gospel as it is for advertising or any other form of today's communication. Fred Craddock, considered one of the dozen best preachers in the English-speaking world, wrote years ago that people will tune out information they think they already have heard, that the gospel is most effective when they "overhear" it. Stories help listeners or readers savor the old "aha!" of discovery of some unvarnished but slightly submerged truth. These days there is even a Network of Biblical Storytellers who practice their craft on each other.

C. William Nichols is one of the best preachers in the Christian Church (Disciples of Christ). And he may be the best storyteller. He still preaches for twenty minutes but, to deal with that ten-minute attention span, he deliberately tries to pack a grabber story or part of one into each five minutes. He preaches with no manuscript, not even notes. Yet his words are so precisely crafted that one thinks each phrase is honed with a delicate literary chisel—which it is. He writes out in full every sermon, word for word. Then he reads and rereads it until it is as close to a memorization as he can get. It leaves him with some catchy phrases, delightful humor, and memorable alliteration—and stories that have the correct length and best words to get the most impact out of the telling.

Not that storytelling is a new art, of course. Jesus was the best. He spun parables and other stories laced with humor, exaggeration, and the most common illustrations and comparisons—things in simple language that spoke directly to real people. That's another key to Bill Nichols' storytelling and to his ministry in general. I have seen him stand outside the church office as ninety children filed out of the nursery en route home, and he addressed each of them by name. These are not nursery kids, or a community ministry, or an audience, but Jessica, Jake, Colleen, and Tony. And that's the first secret of storytelling. The listener is an individual with a name, not part of an audience to be entertained.

As the reader will quickly see in the twelve sermons included here, Nichols speaks to an adult Celia and Bob as readily as he does to Colleen and Tony. And he writes as comfortably as he talks, with powerful stories that relate to individual people's own experiences. The story sermons in this collection all were preached in the 1990s in local worship settings, with the exception of the last one, which is an excerpt of Nichols' sermon at the tumultuous 1991 General Assembly of the Disciples of Christ in Tulsa, when Disciples suddenly turned to this longtime loving and humble local pastor in a moment of crisis and embraced him—to his surprise and the church's credit—as the denomination's general minister and president.

The stories that Nichols tells are from his own experience, true, except that names sometimes are changed when unimportant to the telling. This is not a book from which to draw stories for sermons. Nichols believes one ought to tell one's own.

Robert L. Friedly

Introduction: "Tell Me a Story"

"Tell Me a Story"

It's a request every parent of small children has heard repeatedly: "Tell me a story!" And when the parent honors the request and takes the child onto the parental lap and spins a yarn, the two of them are reenacting a domestic drama that has its origins deep in humankind's history and has been one of the chief means by which the wisdom of the race has been transmitted and preserved from generation to generation.

Early childhood development experts are unanimous in pointing out that telling or reading a story to a child is not only one of the most effective means of bonding between parent and child, it also performs the strategic function of opening the child's learning receptors, to increase the capacity of the child to learn. It is also through this most enjoyable activity that parents pass on to their children the wisdom and precautions that must be learned for life to be successfully lived.

But this desire to hear a story is not left behind when we enter later stages of life. Teenagers buy more movie tickets than any other age group. And the implied demand, when they purchase that ticket and enter the darkened interior of the cinema—popcorn in hand—is "tell me a story." And Hollywood obliges. And whether intended or not, each story related on the big screen teaches life lessons to those watching and listening. Like the hacksaw blade baked into a cake to be given a prisoner, the hidden messages inside the stories depicted on the screen tell the "captive" audience how to be teenagers in the current culture. And their language, their dress, their moral standards, their life expectations have all been served up to them in stories.

While one cannot seriously suggest the kind of censorship that Hitler exercised in the burning of books that articulated philosophies that ran counter to his own, the dictator clearly understood that what youth were reading would profoundly affect their lives and fashion their convictions. It cannot be doubted that the movies and television programs our young people are watching are greatly influencing their view of life. The stories they hear and see are making them what they are and what their world will be.

The power of a story to relay an important message has been utilized repeatedly and with unquestionable result. *Aesop's Fables* have given the entire human race a book of stories whose moral conclusions have become a part of the culture. "The Hare and the Tortoise," "The Dog in the Manger," and "The Fox and the Crow" have become symbols of moral truths that have survived cultural and societal changes. The permanence of humanity's adherence to these simple concepts results not only from their intrinsic truth, but also from the fact that the stories that taught us those truths have become ineradicably lodged in our storehouse of memory.

"Tell me a story" is, in effect, an opening of the mind to truth.

The Bible's Use of Story

Biblical scholars believe that long before humankind found a way to leave a written record of events, storytelling was the means by which the race preserved the concept of God, which had resulted from human experiences in the past. In the dawn of civilization, it was often the responsibility of the oldest member of the tribe to recall events beyond the reach of the memory of most of the members. From parent to child, from grandparent to grandchild, the precious stories of Eden, of Cain and Abel, of Enoch and Noah were passed, each story educating as well as entertaining. And the conclusions drawn from the stories provided the framework upon which a monotheistic religious faith was built.

By the time a written language was developed, one of the first uses discovered for this magnificent invention was the preservation of stories that taught divine truth. Surely one of the earliest was the story that is now our Old Testament book of Job. There are those who insist that Job was a historical character and that the events described actually occurred at a certain time and place. Others believe the story (in the form of a drama) drew on human experience to create an anecdote intended to ask the ubiquitous question, Why do bad things happen to good people? While the story does not provide a satisfactory answer to that question, it demonstrates that such tragic misfortunes do, indeed, happen even to good people. It shows, further, that it is acceptable for us to ask such questions, to express our outrage at such injustices without losing God's love, and that at the end of all our struggles, God is waiting to lavish an everlasting love upon us. The story must often have provided comfort and encouragement to God-fearing sufferers, even as it does today. Neither the story nor the truth it tells has become obsolete.

Another vivid example of a homiletical story is the prophetic book of Jonah. Again, as with Job, there is an endless debate over the historicity of the character of Jonah and the events described in the book that bears his name. It is a genuine tragedy that so much energy has been expended in trying to prove or disprove that a man could be swallowed by a "great fish" and survive the ordeal! That the story is true (in the sense of being true to life) is beyond question. Through the means of a splendid story, several highly significant (and unquestionably true) conclusions may be drawn, among which are these: You cannot run away from God any more than you can run away from yourself; every path that leads away from God leads straight to disaster; there is no place where God cannot be and no human predicament from which God cannot rescue; one cannot lead God; God always reserves the right to be better than we thought God would be; and with God the final word is always love. What a tremendous cargo of glorious conclusions are carried on the shoulders of one small story!

It used to be stated as an absolutely homiletical rule that the preacher should avoid personal references and the relating of personal experiences. Fortunately the biblical writers never heard of that rule. How much poorer we would be if Isaiah had not related the experience of his call to ministry (Isa. 6); or if Jeremiah had not told of his visit to the potter's house (Jer. 18:1–6); or if Hosea had not bared his soul in revealing his heartbreaking experience with his unfaithful wife, Gomer (Hos. 1, 2, and 3). In each of those personal stories, the prophet utilized a vivid and intensely personal experience to teach others the important truth the original event had taught him.

In the New Testament, the apostle Paul splendidly exemplifies the same principle. His conversion experience on the road to Damascus was his story, and he stuck with it. With many similarities, but with some additions, deletions, and changes, he told of that dramatic, personal confrontation with the risen Christ on numerous occasions and to many different audiences and sometimes even to one lone individual. His ministry was based on that personal experience with Christ and what it said to him. And the relating of that experience was the story that he told to the world.

Jesus, the Master Storyteller

Whatever other personal attributes Jesus possessed that attracted the crowds to him, it was surely his uncommon ability to tell stories that was the most appealing to the masses.

Today's preacher, with a carefully monitored electronic speaker system, ideal lighting, a sanctuary specifically designed to draw attention to the one in the pulpit, and a small congregation of like-minded people seated in rows facing the pulpit, cannot begin to understand the difficulties Jesus must have faced in his preaching and teaching ministry. He had to speak wherever the people were—seaside or marketplace, mountainside or small room. Sometimes the crowd was too numerous to be manageable—five thousand or more people on at least one occasion, with malcontents and hecklers interrupting with criticism and condemnation, and favor-seekers clamoring for his personal attention. How on earth did Jesus manage to get his important truths across to the people?

The answer, obviously, is that Jesus told people things they hungered to hear and told them in the common language of the people, frequently telling stories that carried the burden of the message he wanted to deliver. When the scripture reports that crowds followed Jesus' ministry, surely it means that he spoke important truths in ways that invited the interest of the people. And one of the most important tools in that work was his masterful use of stories.

His frequent use of parables is emphasized by Matthew in the words, "And he told them many things in parables" (Mt.13:3); and "Without a parable he told them nothing" (Mt. 13:34–35).

Along with authentic parables (stories told for the purpose of demonstrating a single truth), there are several other examples of picturesque speech that Jesus used with great effect:. There was, of course, the metaphor. "You are the salt of the earth," Jesus said (Mt. 5:13), and "You are the light of the world." (Mt. 5:14). In both instances Jesus likened one entity to another by speaking of it as if it were that article. The qualities known to be possessed by salt and light, Jesus was saying, were also true of his followers. The metaphor was often used by Jesus to criticize the Pharisees, when he spoke of them as "blind guides" (Mt. 15:14) or "whitewashed tombs" (Mt. 23:27–28).

A second kind of picturesque speech frequently utilized by Jesus is the simile. A simile is like a metaphor (that's a simile in itself!) except that instead of saying that something is something else, the simile says that one thing acts like something else.

Examples of Jesus' use of metaphors include his teachings about the lilies of the field (Mt. 6:2 8–29), the children in the marketplace (Mt. 11:16–19), and probably his best-remembered metaphor, the mustard seed (Mt. 13:31–32). In the last example, Jesus says that our faith is like a mustard seed—starting small, but growing, until it finally can accomplish great things.

A third kind of picturesque speech that Jesus used with great effect was the hypothetical situation. "Suppose," Jesus would say, "you should find yourself in such-and-such a situation." Those hypothetical situations to which Jesus referred included being at the altar with a gift for God, and there suddenly remembering that your brother or sister has something against you (Mt. 5:23–24); having your child ask you for a fish or an egg (Lk. 11:11–13); and having one hundred sheep and discovering that one is lost (Lk. 15: 4–7). In each case Jesus gave the listener an opportunity to become a part of the action, taking center stage and mentally acting out the conclusion, thereby learning (through simulated firsthand experience) the wisdom Jesus sought to teach.

Another example of Jesus' ability to use speech in a picturesque manner is the hyperbole. The hyperbole is a deliberate and ridiculous exaggeration used for humorous effect or to emphasize an obvious truth. When Jesus said, "If your eye causes you to sin, pluck it out" (Mt. 5:29), he surely did not intend those words to be taken literally. And who can forget the ridiculous picture of a man with a log in his eye, trying to help another man remove the speck from his eye (Mt. 7:3–5)? Imagine the laughter Jesus evoked by speaking of the Pharisees "strain[ing] at a gnat but swallow[ing] a camel" (Mt. 23:24), or a camel trying to pass through the eye of a needle (Lk. 18:25).

Though they qualify as metaphors, Jesus' self-portraits recorded in John's gospel must have a separate classification as figures, to use the word in the Gospel of John (Jn. 10:6 and Jn. 16:25). In each figure, Jesus characterizes himself by describing himself as a common object: "I am the bread of life" (Jn. 6:35) or "the light of the world" (Jn. 8:12), or "I am the gate for the sheep" (Jn. 10:7), or "I am the vine" (Jn. 15:5). In each case, Jesus describes himself in a figure of speech meant to inform people of his qualities. But surely it is for the parable that Jesus is best remembered.

Jesus and the Parables

The parables of Jesus have become masterpieces of the storyteller's art, for many reasons. They are interesting—frequently suspenseful, with surprise endings. They all depict circumstances that would have been well known to Jesus' audiences, and they all demonstrate predicaments from which human beings need to be released. Who among Jesus' listeners, would not know what it meant to be invited to a wedding, but have nothing suitable to wear? Who would not understand how it felt to be an out-of-work laborer, still hoping at five o'clock in the afternoon to find enough work to take home food for the hungry family? What resident of that agricultural society would not empathize with the farmer whose harvest was threatened by a bumper crop of weeds?

And while the culture in which we presently live may not have had a firsthand experience with some of the "furniture" of Jesus' stories (wine presses, dragnets, buried treasures, etc.), the human experiences indicated by them have not changed. We still need to know how to obtain spiritual security, so that our lives may remain intact even when the tempests come—the aim of Jesus' parable of the house built on the sand, and the house on solid rock (Mt. 7:24–27). We still need to be reminded of the importance of tending to first things first—as Jesus taught in the parable of the wise and foolish bridesmaids (Mt. 25:1–13). And we still need to learn the vital truth that God's dealings with us are not measured by our deserving, but by God's unfathomable grace—which Jesus set forth in the parable of the prodigal son (Lk. 15:11–32).

It was in his parables that Jesus frequently gave expression to his keen sense of humor. Sometimes the humor softened the blow of a stern message he needed to give his listeners. In the midst of a heated controversy about how often one should forgive the offenses of others, Jesus related the marvelous story of the unforgiving servant (Mt. 18:23–35). That story is a splendid example of Jesus' brand of humor—simple, gentle, guileless, inoffensive to anyone. Jesus speaks of a servant (or slave), who owes his king ten thousand talents, or the equivalent of about ten million dollars today. Imagine what laughter Jesus evoked from his audience when he said, "Here is a slave who owes his king ten million dollars!" No one could possibly have owed that much in Jesus' day—let alone a slave! And just listen to what the servant, on his knees before the king, begs for: "Please, sir, have patience with me, and I will pay you everything." A little patience was all he wanted, just to be given a little more time to pay back such a debt. Do you know how much time he needs? At eighty dollars a year (average wages for a working man in Jesus' day) he will need exactly 125,000 years! He was, shall we say, in a bit over his head. Imagine how Jesus' listeners roared with laughter when they heard that story.

Each parable of Jesus sought to set forth one truth. A parable is not the same thing as an allegory, in which each detail of the story has some special significance. A parable teaches one truth.

Without such magnificently memorable stories as "The Good Samaritan," "The Pharisee and the Publican," and "The Prodigal Son," the world's library of stories would be poorer, and the Christian faith would, as a result, be much less well understood.

One Preacher's Use of Stories

Through a half-century of preaching, I have discovered that a good story will say more in less time and be heard and remembered more effectively than almost any other use of words. Through the years, people have often commented to me on sermons they heard me preach in years past and almost always what they remember is a story and truth that it illuminated. In my use of stories in sermons, I have always tried to comply with some basic standards:

While I do not feel that a story must be factual, it must be true to life. And I do not say that a story is true unless it is. I do not report an experience related by another and pretend that it happened to me. I do not tell stories that ridicule or belittle others. I never use a story that is in any way offensive to anyone. I never use a story just to entertain. If it does not speak the truth I want to proclaim, it is a waste of valuable sermon time to tell it. Humor must always be a by-product, never the purpose of telling a story.

I never buy or read books of sermon illustrations. They may be good stories when used by those who wrote them, but my use of them is like trying to walk while wearing some else's shoes. I prefer to find stories in classic literature, in current events, and in my own personal experiences. My life has not been particularly extraordinary, except in ways in which everyone's life is unique and beautiful. But even in my limited experience there have been a multitude of episodes that, if related in a clear and interesting manner, would be worthy of offering as signposts of truth.

I have tried to use a variety of sermonic styles and techniques through the years. I do not use a story in every sermon, and when I do include a story, I do not always use it in the same way as in other sermonic efforts.

I do not "cut and fit" a story to fit the lesson I want to convey. If it does not fit as is, then it should await some later context that would allow it to be itself and fulfill its own purpose.

I do not make use of supernatural phenomena in my stories. God has never spoken to me in a clear, audible voice from heaven. I have never heard the flutter of angel wings, and I have never seen a halo poised above the head of a saintly person. If I ever do, I may tell about the experience in a sermon. But until I do, I will confine my description of events to the terms of my own real experience.

I do not tell stories designed to evoke tears. No dying-mother pleas, no lost-child analogies, no wounded-soldier theatrics for me. Goodness knows, there are enough real tragedies in human life without inventing more that claim no legitimacy other than their ability to make the innocent suffer.

Through the years there have been those kind and supportive listeners who have suggested that I might publish a volume of sermons that include stories. This volume is the result.

1

You Can't Get There from Here

Then Moses went up from the plains of Moab to Mount Nebo, to the top of Pisgah, which is opposite Jericho, and the LORD showed him the whole land: Gilead as far as Dan, all Naphtali, the land of Ephraim and Manasseh, all the land of Judah as far as the Western Sea, the Negeb, and the Plain that is, the valley of Jericho, the city of palm trees, as far as Zoar. The Lord said to him, "This is the land of which I swore to Abraham, to Isaac, and to Jacob, saying 'I will give it to your descendants; I have let you see it with your eyes, but you shall not cross over there.'" (Deut. 34:1–4)

After the death of Moses the servant of the LORD, the LORD said to Joshua the son of Nun, Moses' assistant, "My servant Moses is dead: Now proceed to cross the Jordan, you and all this people, into the land that I am giving to them, to the Israelites." (Josh. 1:1–2)

Slats Broadstock was what would be called "street smart" these days. But in those days of the late 1930s, when I was a child growing up in my hometown, he was simply regarded— with more than a little awe and downright envy—as the one kid in our class who always seemed to *know things*. Oh, not that his intelligence extended to subjects in school, and, in fact, he had already been held back a couple of years, which meant that he was bigger, taller, and more experienced than any of the rest of us. And while we might have known, more than he did, what was the capital of Nova Scotia, how to find the square root of 625, or who wrote "Horatius at the Bridge," Slats Broadstock was the fount of all knowledge in more practical areas. He was the one who knew who was being held in the city jail and why; who was selling contraband moonshine in that prohibition-dry county; what notorious gangsters were at that very moment hiding out in the old cave in Schemerhorn Park; and why Mrs. Ebersole, our teacher, who had always been pencil-thin had suddenly begun to gain considerable girth toward her middle.

Slats's manner in imparting this information heightened the aura of awe and mystery, for he always talked in a kind of conspiratorial whisper, as though what he was telling was known only to a precious few and now this valuable information was being passed on to us. And when we pressed him for details of his latest revelation, he would turn stubbornly silent, as though he had already gone too far in passing on secrets that were entirely too dangerous to be shared.

One morning Slats was waiting for me when I arrived at school. It was the deadline day for book reports, and I had brought my carefully written report of the latest James Fenimore Cooper saga I had read, fully expecting to receive the usual "A" for my efforts. But Slats had read no book and, thus, had no report. And it surely occurred to him that without such a report, he would fail and be held back again. But if Slats's efforts in fifth-grade reading deserved a failing grade, he once again demonstrated his expertise in more practical skills: He offered me a deal. If I would give him my book report, he would tell me how I could get a brand-new bicycle the very next week, at absolutely no cost to me. Who could pass up such a deal? In a matter of moments, my book report, with Slats's name now written in the place where mine had been erased, was in his hand and he was telling me, in a few dramatically whispered phrases, how to get my bicycle. Next week, he told me, Karbe's grocery store would announce a new contest for kids. Whoever brought in the most Hills Brothers coffee can key strips would win a new bicycle. The contest would not be announced until next week, and with this secret knowledge that now only I possessed, I would have the entire weekend to canvass every house in town and gather up all the Hills Brothers coffee can key strips before any other kid knew to ask for them. It was a cinch. I was sure to win!

My parents, however, were skeptical. How, they wanted to know, would Slats Broadstock know of such a thing in the first place and, if he knew, why didn't he hoard up all the Hills Brothers coffee can key strips for himself? (I wisely decided not to tell them what I had traded for this guilty insider information). But early on Saturday morning I began my search for Hills Brothers coffee can key strips. While many families claimed either to use a different brand of coffee, or—for reasons incomprehensible to me—refused to let me paw through their garbage, I did manage to amass a considerable pile of the coveted key strips, and by the end of the day my hands were raw and bleeding from handling the lethally sharp trophies of my scrounging.

Then, for the next several days, I was totally absorbed in guarding them and counting them and recounting them—there were exactly eighty-six of them, definitely enough to win the bicycle, I decided—and in watching for the weekly home-delivered handbill from Karbe's grocery store, which would surely announce, along with the weekly specials on Rinso soap and Ovaltine, the contest that would be my highroad to glory and a new bicycle.

On Wednesday, unable to bear the suspense any longer, I took my collection of key strips in a brown paper bag to Karbe's store after school and looked up the manager. I smugly presented to him my hoard and asked for my justly earned prize. But he only looked blankly at me and said, "There is no contest." I couldn't take it in. "Isn't eighty-six key strips enough?" I asked. "I can go out and get some more!" But he said, "You don't understand. There is no contest. No, eighty-six isn't enough, but eighty-six thousand wouldn't be enough either. There is no contest!"

I don't remember what was said or done next, what attempts I may have made to escape the extreme humiliation and disappointment I suffered in that moment that is forever seared into my memory. But I did carry out of that episode an understanding that was an important asset for my growing up. I learned that there are many wrong roads to any right goal. And no matter how diligently or sacrificially you may travel the wrong road, it simply never reaches the goal. Neither eighty-six, nor eighty-six thousand, nor even eight-six million Hills Brothers coffee can key strips would earn a bicycle. Bicycles had to be earned or bought or won in other ways.

As simple and clear as this truth sounds, it is so desperately hard to get it into our heads, so devilishly difficult to absorb into life. Just see what counterfeit currencies we use in the attempt to buy the prizes we want. We want real, genuine, lasting happiness. But how do we go about trying to get it? Why, by piling up pleasure, of course! And when we can provide enough pleasures for ourselves to pave our lives with them wall-to-wall, genuine happiness will result, right? Well, how many pleasures will it take? Eighty-six? Eight-six thousand? Eight-six million? No, happiness lies at the end of an entirely different road.

Or we want security, the kind of deep and real security that will give us the peace of mind that will allow us to laugh at the time to come. And to get that security we save our money; we lay up much goods in store for years to come. But eighty-six dollars won't buy security; neither will eighty-six thousand dollars, not even eighty-six million dollars. For the evidence suggests that the more we have, the more we need and want; and the more we have, the more frightened we are by the uncertainties and threats of life. It's simply the wrong road to that goal.

Or, perhaps more than anything in this world, you want eternal life, immortality, a place reserved for you in heaven. And to get it, you start tacking up good deeds and good character traits. But how many good deeds and good character traits will that take? Will eighty-six do it, or eighty-six thousand, or eighty-six million? That, too, is the wrong road. You just can't get there from here.

And that is the illuminating, if frightening, conclusion to be drawn from the last episode of the forty-year odyssey of the Hebrew people that we call the exodus, which brought them from slavery in Egypt to the border of the good land that God had promised them. They had grown in this saga in the wilderness; they had become the people of God. Moses had brought down to them, after a forty-day sojourn on Mount Sinai, the law—the Ten Commandments. Here was the foundation stone upon which life must be lived, if it is to please God. And for forty years they had followed that law, lived by it, obeyed it to the letter. Surely they had proved to God their righteousness, and they had thereby earned the right to enter the promised land to possess it.

But what was wrong? Here they were on the very border of that land, but Moses was not leading them over the Jordan River to claim their prize. And as they stood, first on one foot, then on the other, at the very edge of their land, waiting for Moses to lead them into it, Moses was having another of his famous conferences with God. And God was telling Moses that he would not be able to lead the people into their new land. Moses, the father of the Jewish faith, giver of the Jewish Law, had himself been disobedient to God in a small, almost insignificant matter. But since Moses' righteousness was based on obedience to the law, it was that disobedience that made him unworthy to enter the promised land.

So Moses ended his brilliant life in a disappointment. Forty days with God on Mount Sinai obtaining the Ten Commandments had not been enough to win the final victory; forty years of living by the law in the wilderness had not been sufficient to obtain that prize. And since that time there have been forty centuries, but even those forty centuries of obedience to law would not suffice to get you into your promised land. For obedience to law is the wrong currency to buy that prize. You just can't get there from here.

So Moses died and God raised up another leader. His name in Hebrew was Yeshua. In English the name is "Joshua," or, in its Hellenized form, that name is "Jesus." And this Yeshua or Joshua, or the Old Testament Jesus, whose name meant "Savior," was able to take the people of Israel, whose forty years of trying to win a righteousness by obedience to the law had not been able to get them into their promised land, and bring them in at last.

Oh, beloved, do you see what God was saying to the world through this parable of history? You cannot earn your promised land by being good, by obeying all the "thou shalts" and "thou shalt nots" on the books. That's simply the wrong currency. It's like trying to buy a bicycle with Hills Brothers coffee can key strips. You just can't get there from here. No, you can't earn it; you can't deserve it; you can't pay it out on the installment plan of effort or character or obedience. You need a Jeshua, a Jesus, a Savior who *gives* you the kingdom, not through your deserving, but through his.

There is a postscript to the little story with which I began. My humiliating failure to win a bicycle despite all my determined efforts made that autumn a distinctly sad and uncomfortable time for me. I could tell from the awkward behavior of my friends that Slats had bragged to others about his clever deception and how I had fallen for it, hook, line, and sinker. Even the teacher learned of it somehow and compassionately gave me another chance to submit my own book report.

And although they said little about it, my parents surely suffered for me, feeling my humiliation as though it were their own, bearing the cross of my agony and embarrassment. As fall stretched into winter, all my hopes of having a bicycle melted away, like the first snow disappearing under the warmth of an unexpected Indian Summer day.

Then came Christmas morning. And under the tree was a new bicycle for me. Never before had my parents been able to afford such a generous outpouring of Christmas grace. But something prompted them to make what must surely have amounted to a genuine sacrifice in those Depression days, to give me something that I wanted so much to have, but that all my efforts had failed to achieve.

And if today I know the meaning of grace, if today I know the way to heaven, it is because I learned that our promised land can never be won through our own efforts, but only when we are fortunate enough to find a loving heavenly parent who is willing to make some genuine sacrifice to give us what is utterly beyond the reach of our earning.

2
Second Chance

This is the list of the generations of Adam. When God created humankind, he made them in the likeness of God. Male and female he created them, and he blessed them and named them humankind when they were created. When Adam had lived one hundred and thirty years, he became the father of a son in his own likeness, according to his image, and named him Seth. The days of Adam after he became the father of Seth were eight hundred years; and he had other sons and daughters. Thus all the days that Adam lived were nine hundred thirty years; and he died. (Gen. 5:1–5)

But in fact Christ has been raised from the dead, the first fruit of those who have died. For as all die in Adam all will be made alive in Christ. (1 Cor. 15:20, 22)

So far as I am able to recall, the small church in which I grew up had no nursery or kindergarten extended session or any other special provision for small children during the Sunday morning worship service. The tots were expected to sit beside their parents and to *behave themselves,* which meant sitting still and keeping quiet, both of which were next to impossible for me when I was a child. Nevertheless, I did my best, for whether I had actually been told this or not, it was my conviction that God was especially offended by any wiggling or fidgeting in church, and that if I was guilty of any such signs of irreverence, God would surely hold it against me forever. And if—as the stern sermons of those days frequently warned—I should die before the next Sunday, I figured my chances of getting into heaven were entirely dependent upon my behavior at church on my last visit there. So with that much riding on it, I really did try.

I would sit there, unable to see over the hat of the lady in front of me, dangling my feet, which were several inches short of reaching the floor, the circulation in my legs cut off by the front edge of the pew, my mind and my hands itching for some kind of activity. Relief of sorts for this need for activity came in the summertime. In those days before air conditioning came to church, each attender was given at the door a hand fan. Most of these were constructed of stiff cardboard, cut out and printed to resemble a palm leaf, with a sturdy wooden handle. On the back side was printed some message from the merchant who had provided them—usually the local undertaker, whose message boldly proclaimed in black letters, "HARVEY'S FUNERAL PARLOR CARES ABOUT YOU!" And hands that had to be folded in the lap the rest of the year were permitted to flap the fans back and forth, to provide a little respite from the oppressive heat of the Kansas summer.

One year, as I remember, a new-fangled fan was introduced by some progressive merchant for use in the churches. It was a three-piece affair, constructed so that it would fan out for use or fold up when it was not in use. When fully extended, it revealed a picture that usually depicted Jesus praying in the garden of Gethsemane or hosting a dinner party for his disciples. The three pieces of the fan were held together by a brass grommet at the base, surrounding a thumb hole. Those fans were a bonanza to bored youngsters, for they offered so many interesting possibilities for idle hands.

My favorite use for these new fans was to poke my index finger through the thumb hole and see how fast I could twirl the fan. One Sunday morning I got it to twirling so fast it left my finger and sailed past the preacher's head, hitting the leading soprano in the choir right in the middle of her crescendo, thereby making it possible for her to hit the highest note of her entire career.

In fairness I must admit that no one punished me for this breach of ecclesiastical etiquette: no stern reprimand from the pulpit, no "just wait 'til I get you home" threat from my mortified parents, not even a withering glare from the offended soprano. But I was punished all the same. For all through the rest of that service I sat there in my humiliation, thinking that I would give anything—everything—to have that fan back in my hand again. If only I could recall that careless act; if only I could relive that one foolish moment; if only I could start the day over again.

It's a lesson we learn early in life, isn't it, the futility of wishing we could take back a foolish deed or a hasty word. Once done, it's done; once said, it's said; and it can't be undone or unsaid. As Omar Khayyam, the gloomy Persian poet, put it:

The moving finger writes
And, having writ, moves on;
Nor all your piety nor wit can lure it back
To cancel half a line,
Nor all your tears wash out a word of it.

I suspect we have all wished at times that we could have a second chance to undo some wrong that we have done, or to unsay something we said, or to redeem some opportunity we once passed by that never came again.

Surely Adam experienced that yearning: If only he could have a second chance in the garden of Eden to live in harmony with God's will and know once again the perfect serenity of that idyllic place. But no such opportunity was granted to Adam, and there is a terrible sadness about the last chapter of his biblical biography. It closes with the haunting sentence, "Thus all the days that Adam lived were nine hundred thirty years, and he died" (Gen. 5:5). And thus was launched the world that has existed ever since, for all of us: an endlessly repeated pattern of failure and guilt, frustration and futility, with death always coming to put an end to it all, and all our strivings defeated at last by the grim reaper, whose last word finally ends all our hoping and silences all our praying.

Is that depressing enough for you? Is that picture dark enough and grim enough for you to feel, by contrast, the magnificence of the gift God gave the world through Jesus Christ? Isaiah the prophet foresaw the utter relief the world would experience when Christ came to offer us the glory of a second chance. He said, "The people who walked in darkness have seen a great light; those who dwelt in a land of deep darkness—on them light has shined" (Isa. 9:2). For that is precisely what Christ offered the world when he came, the gift that Adam wanted, prayed for, died craving, but was never given: the chance to go back again and reclaim that likeness with God that was stamped upon his soul and to experience the peace, the joy, and the immortality that God intended Adam to have, but which Adam lost forever.

This incredibly good news is the gospel, the kerygma that lights up the New Testament scriptures and makes them read like the "Hallelujah Chorus" on every page. Don't let your familiarity with these words dull your appreciation of the glorious possibilities they try to convey. "So if anyone is in Christ," Paul wrote, "here is a new creation; everything old has passed away; see everything has become new!" (2 Cor. 5:17). Did you hear that? *A new creation:* not just a patched, mended, propped-up improvement of the old, but a new creation.

In the "Family Circus" comic strip that appears in many newspapers, Jeffy is told by his mother to clean up his room, and he asks, ankle-deep in the horrible mess he has made in his room, "Can't I just 'neaten' it up a little?" And all our efforts at self-improvement are little more than that. We have a chronic dissatisfaction with our lives, which is constantly prompting us to try to reform ourselves, to "neaten" up our lives a bit. So we go on diets and exercise regimens, turn over new leaves, make New Year's resolutions, and promise ourselves that we will do better. But despite any good these efforts may seem to accomplish, it's all a bit like straightening up the deck chairs on the Titanic. What we need is new life.

Woody Allen, the comedian and moviemaker, recently published a book of some of his short writings. At the end of his preface, he closed with the wry statement, "The author's one regret in life is that he was not born someone else." I suspect he meant it only as a flippant remark, but there are many people who vainly wish the same thing. But in Christ Jesus we are given that chance.

A man who had achieved some measure of success was recounting his early struggles and hardships as he made his own way in life. He was often called a self-made man. "But," as he put it, "if I had it to do over again, I would call in some help." And that help is precisely what Christ offers us. The self-made man and woman, for all their worldly success and apparent security and momentary pleasures, nevertheless face the day when, being children of Adam, they will go the way of Adam. "As in Adam," Paul said, "all die, so all will be made alive in Christ" (1 Cor. 15:22).

Adam was the progenitor of the life we live in this world, and we are all chips off that old block, experiencing the same weakness in the face of temptation that Adam experienced, the same guilt that haunted him, the same conflicts within us and around us that make us yearn for some Shangri-La, some Eden that seems forever barred to our entrance. But Paul's good news is that if we are in Christ, we are reborn by his power into a new life, a life that no longer carries the stain of sin or the penalty of guilt, a life in which there is peace now and forever and in which death becomes only a minor transition, which finally releases life to find its triumphant homecoming back into that garden where God still waits to give us the fruit of the tree of life.

A few years ago I had occasion to visit Tasmania, the island state just south of Australia. It was discovered by a Dutch ship captain in 1642. The ideal climate and lush vegetation and breathtaking beauty of the place led him to wonder, as he wrote in his ship's log, if he had rediscovered the garden of Eden. A tribe of aborigines lived there, and they were a content and peaceful people who, despite their backward ways, found great happiness in their lush paradise. But soon more explorers (and pirates) came to pillage and steal and kill. The very name the early settlers gave it conveyed what they made of it—Van Diemen's Land (named for the Dutch ship captain, Van Diemen), which soon became "Demon's Land," a homonym that more accurately described what the land had become. The gentle natives were soon all killed off, and the British Empire finally found a practical use for this spoiled paradise. In 1803 it became the "Devil's Island" for the whole British Empire, a penal colony for the most hardened, most incorrigible, most hopelessly unreformable criminals from throughout the British Empire. And when they were sent there, it was with no hope of ever being released or returned to their homes.

A half-century later, the penal colony was abandoned by the British citizens who worked there. It was such a hopeless place and so frightening, and no amount of torture and dehumanizing could keep the prisoners—the dregs of society—under control. When their keepers left them, the prisoners were simply abandoned by the world—hopeless refugees from the bitter result of their own crimes.

But within a few years Christian missionaries went there, despite the dire warnings of those who knew what the grim population was like. The years passed, and finally, when I went there to spend a few days in 1970, I found one of the most gentle, loving, law-abiding, peaceful, Christian places I have ever visited.

It was the story of Eden all over again: A place of beauty and peace, ruined by humankind's sins and failures but made another Eden—a new creation—because Christ came there and gave those people another chance.

And that has been happening in individual human lives everywhere Christ has gone. Through him, human beings, like Adam in their failures and sin and guilt, have been generously, graciously given a second chance, and through Christ, life has come to be Godlike again, a Godlikeness that will last through all eternity.

3

Singular Thanks in a Plural World

Praise the LORD !
Praise God in his sanctuary;
  praise him in his mighty firmament!
Praise him for his mighty deeds;
  praise him according to his surpassing greatness!
Praise him with trumpet sound;
  praise him with lute and harp!
 Praise him with tambourine and dance;
  praise him with strings and pipe!
Praise him with clanging cymbals;
  praise him with loud clashing cymbals!
Let everything that breathes praise the LORD!
Praise the LORD! (Ps. 150)

Whenever I think of unity and diversity, my memories return like homing pigeons to the place where it all began for me.
While I was a senior at Culver-Stockton College, I was also a
student pastor serving my first church, a small but long-suffering
congregation in the tiny Missouri town of LaBelle, which boasted
a total population of 833 souls when everybody was at home.

Despite the sparsity of the population, the town built an abundance of churches. There were six churches in that little town, each valiantly trying to justify its own existence in a strongly competitive demonstration of its sectarian superiority. And almost as if the church builders had accepted the name of the town—LaBelle—as an architectural mandate, every one of those six churches had its own bell. And inasmuch as no church was any farther away than three blocks from any other and all six coexisted in the few square blocks that constituted the village, there was a cacophonous din of bells every Sunday morning and every Sunday evening, as each church summoned its own faithful to worship.

As Thanksgiving approached, I began to visit with the other pastors about the possibility of having a union community-wide Thanksgiving service. Let all the bells of LaBelle join together for once, in a common call to worship, calling all the people together to one service of worship to the one God. So plans were made, a common meeting ground was selected, publicity sent out, and the service was held. It was, in all, a wonderful community-wide service. Well, except for one thing. Of the 833 people in town, 786 stayed home. But all the churches were represented in minimal delegations. There were, as the Baptists delighted in pointing out, a "sprinkling of Methodists" there. And, of course, the Methodists retaliated by sniffing, "Well, we weren't exactly immersed in Baptists either." A handful of Presbyterians came in—decently and in order. Even a couple of Catholics came roamin' in.

I had carefully arranged the worship service to include common forms of worship that I thought would be equally familiar to all present. But I learned my mistake as soon as we began to sing the first hymn, "All Hail the Power of Jesus' Name," and found that while some of us were booming out with the CORONATION tune, others of us were offering the stubborn counterpoint of MILES LANE. And if any angels fell prostrate during the singing of that hymn, it was surely in consternation and frustration.

I figured we were on safe ground at last when we all zeroed in on the Lord's Prayer but the trespasses of the Baptists canceled the debts of the Presbyterians. And when the two Catholics present had said "amen" and sat down, they looked around in stunned surprise as the rest of us droned on with our "kingdom and power and glory."

As it turned out, about the only part of the service that was equally familiar to all present was the passing of the offering plates. But ironically enough, that meager offering of $29.73 led to the sharpest difference of all, for it had not been earlier determined what the offering was to be used for. And in a hastily called conference after the service, the ministers could not agree as to the merits of a single good cause. So in the end it was decided simply to divide the offering among the churches on a *prorated* basis—that is, each church receiving a share of the offering based upon the number of its members who had attended the service. And I fear that the cause of ecumenism in the United States was set back several years, as rigid mathematical formulas began to be enforced (let's see, what is 11/47 of $29.73?).

But despite the faux pas, it was my introduction to the ecumenical movement, an idea whose time had come for me, though of course God had known it all along. And in the intervening years, we have all joined that thrilling adventure to discover that what unites us is infinitely more important than anything that divides us.

It is noteworthy, I think, that this urge to reach out and join in worship with people of other religious traditions has been more frequently demonstrated at Thanksgiving than at any other time. I don't believe I ever participated in a united Christmas Eve service, or a community Easter morning service, though there may well have been such. But there is something in us that reaches out to others and invites the participation of their grateful praise when we lift our hearts in thanksgiving to God. I wonder if it might have something to do with the fact that all the great old Thanksgiving scriptures simply refuse to fit into anyone's cramped, parochial traditions.

Consider, for example, the 100th Psalm. It is probably used at Thanksgiving time more than any other scripture. It begins, "Make a joyful noise to the LORD, all the earth." Now, this psalm was a part of the liturgy of the people of Israel. It was in their hymnbook. It was what they sang in their services. Remember that the people of Israel thought of themselves as an island of truth and reverence in the midst of a sea of paganism. They believed only they—they alone—were the people of God. And God was just as exclusively their God. Their word for "foreigner" and their word for "heathen" was the same. And yet, in writing this hymn, the psalmist had the same feeling that you and I do, that God regards every person everywhere as a beloved child. And for our thanksgiving to God to be complete, it must be a joyful noise lifted up to God by all the lands.

And in the celebrative psalm that is our text—the 150th— there is a joyous outburst of praise that rattles the rafters of our reverence, reverberates through our systematic theology, and sends shock waves through our understanding of what constitutes a community of God's people. Just listen as it builds in force and enthusiasm:

Praise the LORD!
Praise God in his sanctuary.

(Well, so far so good, if we could just agree, for once, on which of the many magnificent temples God's people worship in is really God's sanctuary!)

Praise him for his mighty deeds;
praise him according to his surpassing greatness!

(Well, surely we can't argue with that, for even the most grumbling and picky of us can surely discern the surpassing greatness of the outpouring of God's blessing to us, if only God were a little more selective in his distribution of gifts. For making the sun to shine on the evil and on the just and the rain to fall on the good and the bad appears to us a bit sloppy, as though God is not too good in his aim!)

Then the psalmist summons together the great symphony orchestra and plays this majestic overture of praise to God:

> Praise him with trumpet sound;
>> praise him with lute and harp!
> Praise him with tambourine and dance;
>> praise him with strings and pipe!
> Praise him with clanging cymbals;
>> praise him with loud clashing cymbals!

And then, having reached this fever pitch of joyous abandon in this symphony of praise to God, the organist pulls out all the stops on the great organ and stretches the capacity of our listening hearts to hear this climactic crescendo:

> Let everything that breathes praise the LORD!

Everything that breathes? Yes, everything that breathes is the creation of our God, and for our God to be truly thanked, properly praised, adequately adored, requires a congregation of voices larger than your congregation, or yours and mine together, or all Christians, or all people of religious faith. Everything that breathes must join in this anthem of praise to God.

Now, let me confess at this point that I am in sympathy with you. I know what you're doing. You're sitting there wondering now that I've brought up such a difficult subject, what on earth I'm going to do with it. And, to tell you the truth, I hardly know what to make of this myself. All I know is that for a good many years now this thought has been knocking at the door of my mind, begging for attention, and recently it imperiously knocked down the door and strode in and demanded that I do something with it. Put yourself in my place. What would you do if you were required by your conscience to make something of a psalm that demands, "Let everything that breathes praise the LORD"?

Well, surely we must conclude from this that God regards every person on this planet as a dear and loved child. Some people do not know that yet. Some people may have forgotten it. Some may once have known it. Some may know it, but think it's a distinction that belongs only to them. Some may never know it. But God regards every person on this planet as a dear and cherished child. And God loves them all.

Now, it can be very comforting to us to know that God loves us. We don't have any trouble thinking about that at all. But sometimes it comes as something of a shock to us to realize that God loves other people, too—*all* other people—quite as much as God loves us. God loves the devout and the deviate, the pious and the impious, the saint and the sinner, with the same astonishing devotion. Pope John Paul II and Saddam Hussein, Billy Graham and Charles Manson, Jerry Falwell and Madalyn Murray O'Hare, all share equally in God's love. God cares about Presbyterians and prostitutes, Baptists and bookies, Methodists and murderers, Jews and juvenile delinquents, Catholics and Communists, Americans and anti-Americans with the same passionate intensity that God's son demonstrated on Calvary.

And the frightening conclusion that we are forced by this knowledge to concede is that if our God loves them, then we've got to find some way to love them too.

Somewhere in one of his books, Donald Westlake tells of a woman whose house was being picketed by angry militants during one of the riots of the 1960s. She spent those hours inside her house preparing lemonade and sandwiches for the picketers. Apparently she had heard from someone, somewhere, that she ought to love her enemies. We have heard it too. We've heard it from no less than the Son of God, who loved even those who hammered the nails in his hands and prayed for their forgiveness. Even they, as brutal as they were, as determined as they were to take God's most precious gift to the world and drag it through the muck of shame and the blood of pain, even they were the children of God, and God loved them anyway.

And Jesus, who knew that he was God's child and therefore inherited God's concerns, loved them as well. Jesus spent his entire ministry trying to help people erase those tragic little barriers that people had erected to separate themselves from each other and to rediscover their family relationship with one another, by tracing their spiritual genealogy back to the one God.

Jesus' ministry clearly hammered away at the walls that divide God's people. He spoke freely with the Samaritan woman at the well. She was able to banter with Jesus, where theologian Nicodemus faltered. Jesus praised the centurion, an officer in the hated occupying army, for displaying faith unsurpassed by anyone in Israel. And when Greeks were brought to him during his passion week, he proclaimed, "For this I came into the world" (Jn. 18:37).

And if there is one thing our God would have us do for him, surely it is not just sending God an occasional lacy valentine of worship, though God delights in even that. But can we not learn from the example of God's son, who gave himself in concern, not just for the Jews, not just for those who would one day call themselves Christians, but for everyone, for every creature? That is the thrilling message of Calvary, and of Olivet, where Jesus sent his followers out on that all-inclusive assignment, to tell the good news to every creature! Every creature!

And one day every creature will know that he or she is a child of God and will join this anthem of praise. But whether they know it or not, God does and continues lovingly and generously to be their provider.

Every now and then I think about that wonderful old story by Jean Webster, *Daddy Long Legs.* It was the story of a girl in an orphanage who was befriended by a man who kept his identity unknown. A young bachelor, he was so charmed by this young girl that he maintained for her, across the years, a silent sponsorship. She once saw his shadow, cast from an open office door, and thought of him always afterward in terms of that elongated shadow across the floor—hence her name for him, Daddy

Long Legs. And though she met him often in person, she didn't realize that he was her benefactor. In the years of her maturity, her every need and blessing and opportunity came to her by means of this person in the shadows, whose name she did not know. Of course, that story has a happy ending, a final scene, when she discovers the identity of her benefactor.

But it is when that scene is missing that this story resembles the tragedy of people whose lives have been supported, whose hearts have been nurtured, whose needs have been met, whose mistakes have been buttressed, and whose accomplishments have been made possible by someone in the shadows, whose name they do not know. It is our job to tell them the name of that someone whose name they don't know, the God whose people they are, whether they know it or not. But just as God continues to demonstrate loving parenthood to them until they discover it, so we must continue to demonstrate our brotherhood and sisterhood with them until they realize it.

In the meantime, every worship service is rather like a great choir rehearsal, where we are gathered together to prepare this anthem of praise to God that is scored for everything that breathes. But most of the seats in this choir loft are still empty. And those of us who do come together to sing know how far short our number is.

I once read in a church newsletter that at that church on the following Sunday, "the ladies' trio will sing 'The Hallelujah Chorus.'" Well, maybe praise to God is too great an anthem for us to sing, but sing it we must, because we know who we are and whose we are, and such knowledge makes us sing.

But we know, too, that in this plural world, there are other parts to this anthem and not all of them will be sung in English, not all of them will be sung in Christian, and not all of them will conform to our standards of religious music. But they will all be God's people singing. And I have the feeling that God's music appreciation may be broader than ours.

So let us lift up our hearts and celebrate the goodness of God. And let today's love and understanding and outreaching concern hasten the unity of all God's family, until everything that breathes will join in the doxology of praise:

Praise God from whom all blessings flow.
Praise God, *all creatures* here below.

4

The World Doesn't Care How Much We Know, but the World Really Knows How Much We Care

If then there is any encouragement in Christ, any conso-
lation from love, any sharing in the Spirit, any compassion
and sympathy, make my joy complete: be of the same mind,
having the same love, being in full accord and of one mind.
Do nothing from selfish ambition or conceit, but in humil-
ity regard others as better than yourselves. Let each of you
look not to your own interests, but to the interests of others.
Let the same mind be in you that was in Christ Jesus, who,
though he was in the form of God, did not regard equality
with God as something to be exploited, but emptied himself,
taking the form of a slave, being born in human likeness.
And being found in human form, he humbled himself and
became obedient to the point of death—even death on a cross.
(Phil. 2:1–8)

Oscar Flint was an institution in that small Oklahoma town,
the sort of man everybody knew but nobody would ever claim
as a friend. He was the manager of the only hotel in town and

presided behind the registration desk in the lobby, scowling at the world and greeting guests as though their presence was an unforgivable intrusion.

Since the coffee shop just off the hotel's lobby was the chief gathering place for townsfolk for mid-morning or mid-afternoon coffee breaks, everyone who was anybody came daily under Oscar's baleful eye. Everybody knew his name, but nobody really knew him or, for that matter, cared to. By mutual consent, Oscar and the world just barely tolerated each other, each giving the other the widest possible berth.

One day, when I went to the hotel for my usual morning coffee break, I noticed that a woman was standing at Oscar's place behind the registration desk. When I inquired about Oscar, she told me that he had suffered a stroke. Knowing that he would have no minister—or anybody else, for that matter—to call on him, I asked if I might go to see him. She arched her eyebrows and said, "Well, I'm not sure how he would feel about a call from a minister. He doesn't think too kindly of ministers." It was a fact of which I was already well aware. I had frequently spoken to him and called him by name. But the most he ever gave me in response was an unintelligible grumble.

Nevertheless, I went to Oscar's apartment at the rear of the hotel and knocked at the door. The woman who answered my knock gave me another warning about Oscar's well-known antipathy toward churches and ministers but reluctantly led me to a small, cheerless bedroom where Oscar was propped up in bed.

It was, to be sure, a strained meeting at first. I was scared— a young minister whose training had not prepared me for bearding a genuine atheist in his den. And he was the notorious Oscar Flint, for whom even the most zealously evangelistic churches in town had long since stopped praying.

I cannot now remember a single thing I said or what Oscar said to me in return. I know I had the feeling that I had probably wasted my time in making that call. It did not get any easier the

next few times I called on him. But he seemed to look forward
to those visits. At least, his grumble seemed a bit less threaten-
ing each time I came. But on a Sunday morning a few weeks
later, Oscar spent his first outing after his stroke coming to church.
And at the end of the morning worship service, when I extended
the invitation to Christian discipleship, Oscar Flint came down
the aisle and made his confession of faith.

I would like to tell you that it was my brilliant preaching that
brought Oscar down that aisle, but I know it wasn't. Or I wish I
could report to you that it was the skillful and impassioned witness I made to him when I called on him that produced the
conviction that resulted in his response. But I know that wouldn't
be true either. No, I know what it was: The church had shown
him a little concern, a little softness of heart, a little warmth of
caring through that impromptu call I made on him. I did not
press him hard for a decision, seeking to fulfill my own quota or
to meet the church's evangelism goal. I asked nothing of him. I
simply expressed a little Christian caring for someone whose life
experience was empty of such evidences of concern. And Oscar
Flint told me, one day after that, that my unexpected call was
the first time in his life that he remembered any church reaching out to him to give and not to take.

I learned a valuable truth from Oscar Flint. And I believe
that truth might be expressed in these words: The world doesn't
really care how much we know, but the world really knows how
much we care. In fact, some of the most significant and impres-
sive evidence of the Holy Spirit in us is that our hearts are softened toward the world; we begin to care about those people
around us and are concerned about their needs and feelings, no
matter how they may feel about us and no matter how they
may express those feelings.

I really wish there were some other word to express a quality that is so important and that Paul listed as one of the nine
fruits of the Spirit. The *New Revised Standard Version* translates
this quality as "gentleness" (Gal. 5:23). The *King James Version*

called it "meekness." And though there is a great deal to be said for both of those qualities—and they are both critically needed by a world that often tends to be brutal, violent, and aggressive—neither "gentleness" nor "meekness" really captures the meaning of the Greek word *prautes* in the original manuscript. And because the quality to which that word refers is so very important in our Christian discipleship, I would like to spend a little time illustrating what that word really means.

To do that, I ask you to imagine two horses. First, picture a wild stallion in the mountains of Montana. He was born free, and remains free resisting the efforts of all who would capture him and domesticate him. He gallops down the slope, the sun outlining his finely chiseled muscles, a spray of mane catching the breeze behind his head. His hooves, which have never been shod, furiously pound the dust, and he snorts his disdain for the grazing flocks and herds of domesticated animals. He is arrogant in his independence, haughty in his self-esteem, defiant in his total lack of concern for the wishes of the world. He exists only for himself. The Greeks had a word to describe the quality exemplified by that wild stallion. They called it *hubris,* which we have carried over into our language to express overbearing pride, arrogant self-absorption, being contemptuous of all others.

Now picture another horse, which is so different from the first that they share nothing but the generic classification. This horse has borne so many burdens that his back is now permanently swayed. His spirit has been so broken that he seems totally without temper, and even the children can crawl all over him without upsetting his tranquil resignation. He has worn a harness so often that he feels naked without it. He balks at no burden, resents no command, serves anybody. The Greeks had a word to describe that horse too. They called him *praos*, which is the very quality referred to as the evidence of the Holy Spirit in us. And it does mean gentle and meek, to be sure. But it implies far more than that. I think of it as broken, domesticated, tamed. Now, I don't have to ask which of those horses appeals to you the most. And assuming that you had to be one or the other—though I don't ever recall wishing that I could be a horse of any sort—I suspect you would far rather be the free, wild, untamed, proud stallion up in the hills, than be that plodding, domesticated, lowly bearer of burdens. You'd rather be *hubris* than *praos*. That's the natural person in you talking, because that's the way we all are deep down inside. But when Jesus Christ conquers us and remolds us according to the pattern of his own personality, we become domesticated, tamed, available, useful. And if that doesn't sound very glamorous to you, I'm sorry, but that's the way it was with Jesus Christ, and that's the way it will be with all those who have been transformed into his image.

But there are many people, even many Christian people, who are unwilling to accept this, who continue to live their self-absorbed lives, asking not what they can do for their country (or their church, or their family, or their world), but what their world can do for them, how they can benefit from every human contact. We prefer to listen to that still, small voice within us that insists, "Don't give! Take! Get all you can get while the getting is good. You only go around once in life, so grab all the gusto you can get."

Thomas Alva Edison had a large house in Fort Myers, Florida, with a huge fence around it. Visitors had to push open a heavy iron gate in order to enter the compound and then push it back again until it clanked shut. One of Edison's friend complained to him about the tremendous amount of energy it required to open and shut that gate. With a twinkle in his eye, Edison escorted his friend up onto the roof of the house and showed him an elaborate mechanical device made up of levers and pulleys and pumps. "What you don't know," said Edison, "is that everyone who comes to visit me and opens and closes my gate automatically pumps a gallon of water into my tank up here on the roof."

To be honest about it, we all do the same sort of thing. People come walking into our lives and we resent the intrusion, unless we can figure out some way for that invasion of our privacy to benefit us. We say, "How do you do?" but we really mean, "What can you do for me?" How much water can you pump into my tank? But when Jesus Christ becomes real in your life, a very subtle and profound change takes place, and thereafter you begin to ask not "What can you do for me?" but "What can I do for you?"

Jesus made that clear one day in a conversation he had with two of his ambitious followers, James and John, who were seeking the chief seats in his kingdom. Jesus said to them, "You know that among the Gentiles those whom they recognize as their rulers lord it over them, and their great ones are tyrants over them," (That's *hubris*,) "But," Jesus continued, "it is not so among you" (Mk. 10:42–43a). That is one of the most shocking, one of the most disturbing things Jesus ever said. In that one sentence Jesus completely upset our usual strategy for living, and many of his followers have still not caught on to that. Many people who claim Jesus as Lord still do not realize how strictly Jesus demanded that His followers must march to a different drummer and get out of step with the world.

Then Jesus went on to amplify his teaching: "Whoever would be great among you must be your servant, and whoever would be first among you must be the slave of all. For the son of man came not to be served, but to serve, and to give his life a ransom for many" (Mk. 10:43b–45). And in those words, Jesus revealed the reason why he is so revered by the world, and followed by millions of devoted disciples: because he was the most useful person who ever lived. His greatness was found in his vulnerability, his willingness to serve, his availability to everyone who had a need.

On the occasion of the seventy-fifth birthday of Albert Schweitzer, a reporter from *Life* magazine went out to his jungle mission to interview him. The reporter found him down on his hands and knees on the floor of a hospital room, scrubbing the floor, cleaning up after one of his patients. The reporter, repelled by that disagreeable task, told Dr. Schweitzer, "I wouldn't do that for a million dollars." And the good doctor replied, "Neither would I."

But something beyond the reach of a million dollars controlled Albert Schweitzer. It was the spirit of the one who "though he was in the form of God, did not regard equality with God as something to be exploited, but emptied himself, taking the form of a slave, being born in human likeness. And being found in human form, he humbled himself, and became obedient to the point of death—even death on a cross. Therefore God also highly exalted him and gave so him the name that is above every name, that at the name of Jesus every knee should bend, and every tongue confess that Jesus Christ is Lord"(Phil. 2:6–11).

And so God will exalt all those who, because of the spirit of Christ, humble themselves to become servants—tamed, domesticated, available, useful. For as he promised, "Blessed are the meek"—the gentle, the *praos*, those who are willing to be everyone's servant—"for they shall inherit the earth."

5

Commitment That Counts

As they were going along the road, someone said to him, "I will follow you wherever you go." And Jesus said to him, "Foxes have homes, and birds of the air have nests; but the Son of Man has nowhere to lay his head." To another he said, "Follow me." But he said, "Lord, first let me go and bury my father." But Jesus said to him, "Let the dead bury their own dead; but as for you, go and proclaim the kingdom of God." Another said, "I will follow you, Lord, but let me first say farewell to those at my home." Jesus said to him, "No one who puts a hand to the plow and looks back is fit for the kingdom of God." (Lk. 9:57–62)

In the home in which I grew up, playing cards were unknown. We had Flinch, Rook, Old Maid, Authors, and other card games, but at that time and place, cards with "spots," as we called them—the "spots" being spades, hearts, clubs, and diamonds—were as assiduously avoided in the homes of proper God-fearing, church-going people as were liquor and pornography. I never quite understood the reasoning behind the banning of playing cards, especially since the evils to which they were said to lead could just as easily have occurred in the use of Flinch, Rook, or Authors—at least, it seemed so to me. But that absence in the home of my childhood may account for the fact that I never learned to play poker. For if anyone ever figured out a way to play poker with Old Maid cards, I never heard of it.

But like all forbidden things, the game of Poker always held a strange and compelling fascination for me. And even today the feature I remember most vividly about the old Western movies, which were the staple Saturday afternoon entertainment for me and my friends when I was growing up, was not the shoot-out between the cowboys and the cattle rustlers or the daring daylight robbery of the stage coach, but the dramatic showdown at the poker table in the saloon. It always started as a friendly game with six or eight men participating. One by one the bit players threw in their hands with such highly original pieces of dialogue as "It's too rich for my blood!" or "I fold," until only two players were left, facing each other across the table: the hero in his white hat, and the villain, who always seemed to be named Black Bart, the name derived from the traditional color of his wardrobe. The hero was, for some reason, usually called "Tex," whether he was from Texas or not. One cowboy called Tex was asked if he was from Texas, and he said, "Naw, I'm really from Louisiana, but I'd a whole lot rather be called 'Tex' than 'Louise'."

But, back to the poker game in the old saloon. The air becomes electric with excitement and suspense as the piano player stops playing "Red River Valley" to join the others watching transfixed, looking from the hero to the villain like the spectators at a tennis match. Finally the climactic moment arrives when Black Bart slides all his remaining stacks of poker chips to the center of the table. The hero responds by pushing in his remaining chips, saying, "I'll see you." Then he removes a legal paper from his ten-gallon hat, lays it on the table, and says, "And I'll raise you with this deed to the ranch!" Gasps all around the table punctuate the dramatic moment, no one thinking to asking the hero how he happened to be carrying the deed to the ranch in his hat in the first place.

Finally, Black Bart says, "I call," and smugly plunks down his "full house"—one eyed jacks over eights—and starts to rake the pot into his corner. But the hero calmly lays down his hand to show that he has drawn a royal flush, thereby winning the game, the pot, the girl, the ranch, and a contract for six more "B" pictures at Universal Studios.

Now, if I have misinterpreted the action or misused the vocabulary of a poker game, please forgive me. I told you I never learned to play the game! And I hope you will not quote me as saying that the Christian life is like playing poker! Nevertheless, there is a certain aspect of a poker game that is really illustrative of the kind of commitment that is required in our discipleship. For if I understand the strategy of poker, two things are necessary to be a winner. You must have a good hand, and you must believe in that hand so strongly that you are willing to commit something to that belief. You have to be willing to put something in the pot to prove your belief. It costs you something to win at poker. You have to risk something of yourself. And the winner is not always the one who has the best hand. Those who fold early, throwing in their hand and leaving their chips for others to win, may have had the best hand, but they were afraid to risk anything on their belief that what they had was a winner.

As inelegant as this metaphor may seem to you, it occurs to me that many Christian people have "thrown in their hand" insofar as their faith is concerned. When asked to demonstrate the seriousness of their belief in Jesus Christ as Lord of their lives and the sincerity of their dedication to him by offering various evidences of commitment, they apparently feel that their belief is not certain enough to justify such an investment, so they give it up.

Let me ask you: Do you really believe that Jesus Christ was (and is) a unique person with a uniquely special relationship with God, which permits him to offer you forgiveness of sins and salvation of your soul and the promise of eternal life? You once accepted Jesus Christ as your Lord and Savior. Do you still believe that? Then what are you willing to give of yourself to demonstrate and confirm that belief? Or at the first hint of sacrifice, the first call for the confirmation of your faith by some work of Christian witness and service, are you ready to throw in your hand?

An old hymn parody depicts this kind of shallow conviction that shrinks from any call to service or sacrifice:

I'll go where you want me to go, dear Lord;
    Real service is what I desire;
I'll sing a solo any day, Lord,
    But don't ask me to sing in the choir!

I'll say what you want me to say, dear Lord;
    I want to see things come to pass,
But don't ask me to teach girls and boys, dear Lord,
    I'd rather just stay in my class.

I'll do what you want me to do, dear Lord;
    I yearn for the kingdom to thrive;
I'll give you my nickels and dimes, dear Lord—
    But please don't ask me to tithe.

I'll go where you want me to go, dear Lord;
    I'll say what you want me to say;
But I'm busy just now with myself, dear Lord—
    I'll serve you some other day.

(author unknown)

Unfortunately, as the rapid spread of communism earlier in this century demonstrated so vividly, wrong ideas strongly held can often defeat right ideas weakly held. And that's why I worry about the future of Christianity in this world. Not that Christianity is a wrong idea. It is, on the contrary, the best idea, the noblest set of truths ever set forth in this world. But we who have been given that right idea hold it too meekly, too weakly to give it the power that it deserves.

I was fascinated a few years ago by the frightening accounts of how the book *The Satanic Verses*, by Salman Rushdie, was opposed by the Muslim world. The book denies that Mohammed, the founder of Islam, was the divine son of God, that he had any supernatural authority or power, or that the book he gave the world (the Koran) was the divinely inspired word of God. And just see how the Muslim world reacted to what they saw as blasphemy against their religion! Immediately a multimillion-dollar reward was offered to anyone who would murder the author. Gigantic rallies were staged in Muslim countries around the world, protesting not only the book and its author, but the countries of England (where the author was said to be hiding), and the United States (where Rushdie was scheduled to make a lecture tour).

So strong and so unified was the active opposition to the book and its author that security was tightened in airports all around the world. Even in our country, where freedom of speech and freedom of the press are cherished rights protected by the first amendment to our constitution, the two largest chains of bookstores removed all copies of the book from their shelves. Meanwhile, in several Muslim countries, suicide squads were trained to accomplish the assassination of the author, even at the willing cost of the lives of the killers, who would be regarded as holy martyrs for their effort.

Now think of the power of that religion! No wonder Islam is growing rapidly throughout the world and even now hundreds of Muslim missionaries are at work in many countries, including the United States of America. But here is the point: Where does that power come from? Not from the religion to its adherents (and I am not ready to accept the superiority over Christianity of any religion that urges its adherents to commit murder and other acts of terrorism). No, the power demonstrated in all this is the power that comes from its adherents to their religion. What they are willing to give for their faith, what they are willing to commit to their religion empowers their faith. It is the power of *individual commitment*.

But here is what really gives me pause about all this: The three things Salman Rushdie is accused of saying in his book against Mohammed that have galvanized the whole Muslim world to take murderous action are the three things countless authors have been saying for years against Jesus Christ. The bookshelves are full of volumes that deny the divine lordship of Jesus Christ, disclaim the supernatural power and authority that Jesus demonstrated, and repudiate the divine inspiration of the Bible as the Word of God. And where is the Christian world demanding the recanting of such lies? Where is the power of Christians to combat the rising tide of filth and immorality openly displayed in movies and television programs that diametrically contradict Christian values? Where is the power of Christians to protest the sleazy and inaccurate lampooning of the Christian religion that is frequently the only way the Christian religion is depicted on television? Our voice has become so weak, so small, and so disunited that we cannot make anyone listen. We cannot even defend ourselves.

And it isn't that there aren't enough Christians in our country. Polls continue to insist that more than ninety percent of the people in this country claim to believe in God and that almost three fourths claim to be Christians. It isn't that there aren't enough Christians; but apparently such Christians as there are are not Christian enough. We may be many, as Will Rogers would say, but we sure ain't much!

I have the distinct feeling that Jesus is displeased by such an insipid, weakly held faith, and I believe that he wants no part of such uncommitted disciples. And the reason I believe that is that our scripture reading depicts Jesus denying membership to three applicants who came to him, waiting to be admitted to his group. The first man sounded like an ideal candidate. He approached Jesus enthusiastically and said, "I will follow you wherever you go!" But Jesus simply told him what his discipleship would involve. He said, "Foxes have holes, and birds of the air have nests, but the son of man has nowhere to lay his head." In other words, are you sure you want to follow me, when I cannot promise that you will always travel first class and stay in nice, four-star hotels? Apparently, faced with this warning, the vapid candidate turned away.

The second seemed eager to follow Jesus, if Jesus was willing to fit into his busy schedule. "Lord," he enthused, "I will follow you—and very soon, too. But first I have more important things to do. I must first bury my father." Not that his father was already dead and just awaiting funeral arrangements to be made. No, what this young man was saying was, "I couldn't possibly leave right now. My family is depending upon me. But someday, when all my family members are dead and buried, then—unless something else intervenes, of course—I will follow you."

The third applicant for discipleship had only a single qualification: "Let me first say farewell to those at my home." That certainly seems reasonable. But again, apparently this eager but shallow candidate for discipleship had something more in mind than just a simple farewell. What he meant was, "Someday, Lord, I'll look you up and follow you. But first I have these other interests and responsibilities, and I can't just let them go. Someday, Lord, I'll be there right where you are. But in the meantime, don't call me, Lord. I'll call you."

But Jesus turned away all these people, for one single reason: He will not be our Lord unless we are willing to lay all that we are and have before his throne. It will cost you something to be a Christian. But have you considered what it will cost if you aren't?

Now that the Roman Catholic Church has revised its catalogue of saints and left out of its list Patrick, the patron saint of Ireland, I don't know what to call him. Brother Patrick, I guess. But for those of you who admire that historical religious leader (as I do) and still want to think of him as a saint, rest assured that he was a saint, as the New Testament uses that word. As a matter of fact, so are you, dear reader!

One of the beautiful stories told about Patrick relates that when he was an old man, he once led a tribal chieftain to Christ. As he led the old chief into the waters of a river for baptism, Patrick carried with him the tall iron cross to signify in whose name the baptism was being performed. When they got to the middle of the river, Patrick thrust the sharp-pointed end of the cross into the bed of the river, to stand it there while he baptized the chief. But his eyesight was very poor and, unseeing, he thrust that sharp point through the foot of the old chief, who stood unflinching. Only when the saint saw the crimson in the water did he realize what a shocking thing he had done. And he said, "Oh, my son, why did you not cry out?" "Why should I cry out?" asked the chief. "I supposed it be part of the baptism."

In the face of such a willingness to sacrifice for our faith, can we see how we must surely insult Christ by offering him a faith that shrinks from any pain or any sacrifice of pleasure or convenience?

A discipleship that costs you nothing will be worth nothing to you. But every day there will come some opportunity for you to strengthen your faith and give it wings by increasing your commitment. That opportunity may come disguised as a demand for sacrifice, witness, service, generous giving, or valiant forgiveness. But in every case, it is a moment when a deeper commitment is possible, making your faith more valuable to Christ and to yourself.

6

Thou Preparest a Table before Me

You prepare a table before me
in the presence of my enemies;
you anoint my head with oil;
my cup overflows. (Ps. 23:5)

When the hour came, he took his place at the table, and the apostles with him. He said to them, "I have eagerly desired to eat this Passover with you before I suffer; for I tell you, I will not eat it until it is fulfilled in the kingdom of God." Then he took a cup, and after giving thanks he said, "Take this and divide it among yourselves; for I tell you that from now on I will not drink of the fruit of the vine until the kingdom of God comes." Then he took a loaf of bread, and when he had given thanks, he broke it and gave to them, saying, "This is my body, which is given for you. Do this in remembrance of me." (Lk. 22:14–19)

In the days when I was a student minister—which meant full-time student, part-time minister, besides also being the part-time custodian and only secretary of the church I served—I was also a bachelor, and my skills in preparing food fell considerably short of matching my enjoyment in consuming food.

Fortunately the members of that small church were sensitive to my predicament, and many of my memories of that time recall occasions when a table was prepared before me.

I well remember one Friday when, as usual, I was very busy. The bulletin for Sunday had to be mimeographed, and, as the church's only secretary, I had to do it. But the grate had fallen out of place in the furnace, and someone had to crawl inside the cold furnace and carefully replace the grate in time to fire it up before the Sunday services. And since I was also the part-time custodian, I knew that it was my job. Also there was a sermon to write and a paper to prepare for a class I was taking. In addition to all that, I received a message that one of the elderly ladies of the church wanted to see me.

Leaving all the more urgent tasks for a while, I turned my '35 Chevy down the street where Mrs. Hattie Marie Sheridan Bilowsky Previn lived. (And oh, how she loved for me to repeat all those names, as though each were a royal title!) "I can make a quick call on her before lunch," I thought to myself as I neared her Victorian house—like herself, a gracious but fading relic of a more august era. But I should have known. A "quick call" on Hattie Marie Sheridan Bilowsky Previn was most assuredly a contradiction in terms.

She showed me into her parlor, where she indicated a large, upholstered wing-back chair armed with a crocheted antimacassar and matching arm covers. "You'll be comfortable here," she told me, "while I put together a little lunch." I protested, listing all the important things that demanded my attention that day. "Nonsense!" she interjected. "I don't care if you are a minister, you have to eat." I started my rebuttal by reminding her that I wasn't yet a minister, but my voice trailed off as I realized I was talking to her back, as she disappeared into her kitchen.

"Please don't go to any trouble," I begged, my last shot fired in a losing battle. Asking Hattie Marie Sheridan Bilowsky Previn, whose whole life had been spent in making virtues of necessities, not to go to any trouble would be like asking the sun not to shine, or the tide not to come in. The extravaganza of preparing a meal for company had begun, and she would not be distracted from it. I heard the comforting sounds of kitchen utensils being put to their intended use, then I began to detect the preliminary aromas of food being prepared.

Leaving the food to the ministries of her wood-burning range, she appeared in the dining room to continue her preparation, giving me the opportunity to reiterate my plea, "Please don't go to any trouble." But she ignored my remark as she withdrew from an ancient rosewood china cabinet lustrous crystal glasses and heavy china plates and cups—probably wedding gifts, I thought. Gleaming silverware joined the crystal and china pieces in careful precision on the dining table.

"I really wish you wouldn't go to so much trouble," I pressed her, but she was off to the kitchen again. I relaxed in the wing-back chair, as the kitchen fragrances began to tickle my nose: made-from-scratch biscuits browning, pork chops sizzling in the iron skillet, applesauce with cinnamon sticks sending its tantalizing message to my hunger. The longer she spent laboring over the preparation of her meal, the more glad I was that I had lost my debate with her. Finally, as she touched a lighted match to the candles that graced the center of the table, she announced, "Well, such as it is, it's ready."

With a courtly grace that attempted to match her own, I seated her before I took the place she had indicated as mine: "Mr. Previn's place," she called it, although Mr. Previn had long since relinquished his claim on the chair and everything else that he once had called his own in this world. "Would you ask the blessing?" she asked. I would and I did. Then, while I savored each mouthful of the delicious meal, I noted that she gave more attention to my eating than to her own. "I have never felt lonely," she said, "except at mealtime. Meals were meant to be shared. And when you've no one to share food with, it's almost more trouble than it's worth to cook. But when you have the blessing of sitting down to share a meal with someone you care about, it's almost a religious experience—almost like the sacrament of the Lord's supper at church, and our Lord himself is present in the midst."

I was a little late that day in getting back to the duties that called me. But I knew, when I saw the tears in the eyes of Hattie Marie Sheridan Bilowsky Previn, as I finally wrenched myself away from her house, that I had been celebrating something very much like a sacrament. In preparing a table before me, she had become a partner with the divine. And in sitting at that table, eating the food she had prepared, I knew that I had received gifts that represented the grace of God.

I wonder if you have noticed how throughout the Bible the eating of food was often inseparably connected with religious experiences. The Passover celebration was a symbolic meal, through which a Jewish family recalled God's deliverance of Israel from bondage. And likewise the Feast of Weeks, the Feast of Tabernacles, and other great religious festivals were all, as their names suggest, feasts. Even the weekly Sabbath observance began with a family meal.

When Jesus came, he emphasized this relationship between faith and food. A common criticism leveled against him was that he came eating and drinking—that is, he frequently enjoyed the fellowship of a meal, even with those whom the super-pious regarded as unfit for companionship with him. He even compared himself with food, to show that our souls need him as desperately as the body needs nourishment. "I am the bread of life," he said (Jn. 6:35).

All this is suggested by the line of the Twenty-third Psalm that says (in the familiar King James version): "Thou preparest a table before me in the presence of mine enemies." When a shepherd took his flock out into the fields for grazing, he knew from experience that the sheep would be instinctively trusting him to provide safe places for their grazing. Not all pastures were safe. Some contained poisonous plants that would be fatal to the sheep if eaten. Also, there were plants whose sharp thorns would penetrate the soft noses of the sheep and cause ugly sores. So the shepherd of the sheep went ahead of them, uprooting these enemies of the sheep, and would pile them up and burn them. Thus, the pastures were made safe for the sheep to graze. The pasture became, as it were, a table prepared for them.

And this line of the Twenty-third Psalm suggests to us that God accepts the responsibility of providing for us the food and all the other resources we need, which will safely nourish our bodies and our souls.

When the gospel of Mark relates the story of Jesus' feeding the multitude of five thousand hungry people, it says that Jesus performed that miracle because when he looked out over that multitude, "he had compassion for them, because they were like sheep without a shepherd" (Mk. 6:34). Sheep without a shepherd would have no one to lead them into safe pastures, no one to provide food for them.

On the day when Jesus made that remark, he assumed responsibility for feeding that vast multitude of people. He was God's representative. He was here on God's behalf, laboring among people who accepted him as God's messenger. No wonder he felt that it was his responsibility—and the responsibility of his helpers—to provide food. Because God has always accepted and fulfilled that responsibility in one way or another, we must be willing as God's followers and helpers to share that burden.

When a Jewish family bows their heads for the grace before a meal, the prayer of thanks is usually this one: "Blessed art Thou, O Lord God of Israel, who bringeth forth bread from the earth." And though that process of "bringing it forth" has in recent years become so complicated that it is no longer easy for us to trace it, every bit of food we consume has been brought forth from the earth through the processes of God's design. Maltbie Babcock, the poet, took the time to trace that process in his little poem:

Back of the loaf is the snowy flour,
Back of the flour, the mill;
Back of the mill is the seed and the shower,
And the sun, and the Father's will.

And it is the Father's will that your needs should be met. The miracle of the manna in the wilderness was testimony to that. Those who followed the leadership of God learned that they could count on God to prepare a table before them. Is it any wonder, then, that God's followers have through the ages taken the lead in providing bread for the hungry people of the world? On that day when Jesus faced the multitude of five thousand hungry people, he startled his disciples by demanding of them, "You give them something to eat" (Mk. 6:37). It was a divine command, a summons to represent God in doing what God has promised to do for the world: He will prepare a table before us.

It has been heartening that in recent years many people not connected with the church have rallied to the problem of world hunger. Through such programs as "Live Aid," "Band-Aid," and "Hands Across America," many people have become involved in ministries of compassion to provide food and other material to help needy people across the world. Those programs have been widely publicized and glowingly praised—and rightly so! But even though unheralded and frequently overlooked, the churches of our country have continued every year, year after year, to give many times as much food to the hungry in all parts of the world as has been given in all these much-publicized efforts. And it is because we accept our role as disciples of the Christ who bids us, "You give them something to eat."

But there is another understanding of this line of the Twenty-third Psalm that we must not miss. As Christians, we understand that the table that has been prepared before us is the Lord's table, which provides for us the bread of life, without which our souls would die.

To be sure, there is a holy mystery that surrounds our celebration of the sacrament, a mystery that we can neither fully understand nor explain. Through the ages there have been some ridiculous efforts at explanation. One common belief, generally accepted in the superstitious medieval years, was that the bread and wine, when consumed by a believer, actually became—molecule for molecule—the body and blood of Christ. This was regarded by people in those days as powerful magic! Just imagine: The priest says a few magical words over common bread and common wine and—presto chango—they become something entirely different! And what were those magic words? Those words that Jesus spoke of the bread, "This is my body," became, when translated into Latin, *"Hoc est corpus meum."* So, attempting to imitate the sound of those Latin words, *"Hoc est corpus meum,"* the people would say, attempting to create a little magic on their own, "Hocus pocus!" Is there magic here?

No, not magic, but mystery: The bread and cup become something more than common food and drink, when they are shared in remembrance of a living Christ, whose *presence* becomes real to us in the fellowship of the table. And while those of us whose modern affluence relieves us of the anxiety of wondering where our next meal is coming from gather at the table, we seek not the bread for our bodies, which provides temporary strength and nourishment for today; we seek bread for our souls, which provides the spiritual strength and nourishment that will last forever.

Many years ago I heard one of our pioneer missionaries tell of those bleak days when he was one of the first Christian missionaries to settle among a people who knew nothing about Christ. He often felt alone, unprotected, and spiritually depleted as he went about a task that seemed so unpromising at first. But although he was the only Christian in a large settlement of people in that undeveloped country, he continued every Sunday to celebrate the sacrament of the Lord's supper all by himself. One

Sunday, a small boy of the village watched him through the window of his hut as he took the small amount of bread and the tiny drink of wine. The boy, mistaking the ritual for a midday meal, said to him, "Mister must not be very hungry today." And the missionary replied fervently, "Hungrier than you'll ever know."

So each of us comes to the Lord's table with hungers that no one knows but us: we hunger for acceptance, for forgiveness, for wholeness, for patience, for strength, for hope, for peace. And Christ's presence feeds us. He is the host and he is the bread. All about us in life are enemies that would seek to destroy our souls. But here, as I discovered at the table of Hattie Marie Sheridan Bilowsky Previn so long ago, when this food is shared in Christ's name, he is present. And because he loves us and has assumed the responsibility of giving us whatever we need, he prepares a table before us.

7

Mr. Smith Goes to Heaven

Then I saw a new heaven and a new earth; for the first heaven and the first earth had passed away, and the sea was no more. And I saw the holy city, the new Jerusalem, coming down out of heaven from God, prepared as a bride adorned for her husband. And I heard a loud voice from the throne saying, "See, the home of God is among mortals. He will dwell with them as their God; they will be his peoples, and God himself will be with them; he will wipe every tear from their eyes. Death will be no more; mourning and crying and pain will be no more, for the first things have passed away. (Rev. 21:1–4)

Mr. Smith went to heaven this week. It was a pleasant journey, despite all the worry and dread that had preceded it and notwithstanding the pain and pressure of all the preparatory details. Those whom he left behind, seeing only his departure, missed the whole point of the event. "It was so sudden, so unexpected, such a tragedy," they said among themselves, and all nodded solemnly, as though no one could possibly disagree. But Mr. Smith knew that it was neither sudden nor unexpected, and not even a tragedy—except maybe for those whose judgments

are so anchored to the here and now that they cannot conceive
of anything they can't see as real.

And certainly it was not unexpected. Ever since that time
when Mr. Smith was a small lad and his dog's demise had given
him his first glimpse of that inevitable experience of all life, he
had known that death is the most expectable of all our experiences. "Death and taxes," someone had said, the two great inescapable events in this life. But even taxes can be adroitly avoided.
Loopholes can be found by those whose cleverness exceeds their
scruples. And some people are literally too poor to be bothered
with taxes. But death yields to no clever bargaining, no importu-
nate dickering. It is patient, but undeniable.

Mr. Smith had occasionally encountered death, but mostly
as a vague realization of something that invariably happened to
someone else. The bad guys in the black hats in the cowboy
movies of his childhood bit the dust. Period. No tears there—not
even a fleeting regret or a momentary thought of what it actually meant. But how different it was when his grandfather died!
He was shown a figure—like a department store dummy lying
down in a box that had been upholstered to make it look like a
sofa. They told him it was Grandpa. Nonsense! Grandpa was
long-winded stories and a patient lap for crawling up into, and
slow walks through the neighborhood, and a deep chuckle over
childish pranks, and homemade tops and toys and whistles and
birdhouses, and a million ideas for having fun on a rainy afternoon. That still figure in the box was not Grandpa, though there
was some resemblance.

And though they told him that Grandpa had gone to heaven,
they suddenly began to speak of him—very self-consciously—
only in the past tense, as though Grandpa hadn't simply gone
somewhere, but had suddenly, somehow, ceased to exist. It was
a real puzzle for a small boy.

But there were other things to think about and to do. Life
was what was real, and he celebrated it in an endless succession
of days and nights, with their excitements and adventures and

delights, their pleasures…and their pains. Then one day he was a man and exchanged the carefree joys of childhood for the responsibilities of adulthood. There were choices to be made, and he made them: It was more important to be honest than to be rich; more desirable to be loving than to be domineering; more satisfying to live by principles than to live for pleasures.

But even more important, he chose Christ as the polar star of his life, chose to believe that Christ's resurrection from the dead had something genuine and personal to say to him about his own life—and his own death. So he became a Christian. Not a perfect one, certainly, and his prayers for forgiveness along the way were as frequent as they were fervent.

As life lengthened, his exposure to death became more common. The obituary page of the newspaper began to be more interesting to him than the noisy headlines of the front page. And as each companion of life's way walked on ahead of him, leaving him standing here alone, earth became more and more lonely and heaven seemed less remote.

Besides the loneliness, there were other problems that made life here less pleasurable as the years succeeded each other. Stiffened joints and weakened eyes and a multitude of miscellaneous pains and problems created a collusive, concatenated chorus of complaints for which earth held no balm.

But as his body declined, his soul achieved a certain renaissance. There was time now for reading the Bible, for pondering life's mysteries, and for prayer. Indeed, his conversations with heaven seemed to become more meaningful and more informative than his conversations with the earth. And the nearer he came to life's ultimate destiny, the less forbidding it looked. Then one night this week, heaven touched earth briefly, and Mr. Smith slipped through that confluence and found himself in heaven.

I wish Mr. Smith were writing these words to you, to tell you about that extraordinary journey and the vital, incredibly happy life he now lives in heaven. But our ears and minds are equipped only for the understanding of this world. He could not tell us if he were here, and if he told us we could not understand. Those few who have made the journey to heaven and back have found it frustrating and futile to try to explain what happens to us when the world says that we have died. Jesus didn't even try, but contented himself only with telling his listeners that whatever they hoped heaven was, however extravagantly they might have imagined its joys and riches, it was far beyond their highest expectations.

Lazarus, who was called back from death in Jesus' most spectacular miracle, was strangely silent following his return. Legends say that Lazarus spent the rest of his second span in this world in the silence of unrelieved sadness: sadness because he had found it necessary to relinquish his existence there to return to earth to provide a living proof for those who were slow to believe Christ's power over death, and silence because he simply could find no words to describe the ineffable beauty of the life that awaits us.

John, the aged seer who wrote the Book of Revelation, had a vision of heaven, but felt the same constraints of the earthly limitations of language and understanding in attempting to record for posterity what he had seen there. So he used signs and symbols—golden streets and jasper walls and gates of pearl and crystal seals. And there are times when symbols are the closest we can come to expressing reality. Poets have understood this. So Robert Burns said:

> My love is like a red, red rose
> That's newly sprung in June.
> My love is like a melody
> That's sweetly played in tune.

And it would be irreverent and unnecessary to point out to the poet that his lady fair didn't really look like a red rose or a lilting melody. But the feeling was expressed in those symbols and expressed truly.

So we must resort to the use of symbols and signs to describe what Mr. Smith found in heaven. And I must beg you—as I beseech God—to forgive my clumsy human limitations that require the use of such childish similes and metaphors. It's the best I can do.

First of all, Mr. Smith found the experience of death painless, untroubled, and serene. And for this fact we have medical and scientific evidence. A score of books published in recent years report numerous case histories of people who have been literally snatched from the jaws of death by some extraordinary medical measures. People who have been dead—literally dead—for several minutes have been restored to life. And the vast majority of them returned to life sadly, having been eager to continue the new experience into which they had been introduced. Those interviewed have spoken of being met by someone—a loved one who had gone on ahead of them or some kind and loving new companion whom many identified as Christ. But the overwhelming scientific evidence indicates that Mr. Smith found the passage painless, untroubled, and serene.

But from this point we must leave the conclusions of science and venture on in faith to follow Mr. Smith in the odyssey of his soul. These are not my imaginings, however, but the assurances of the Holy Scriptures.

As Mr. Smith entered heaven, he found that he was known there, that his new host had been expecting him, and that his place was ready and waiting for him. And in that instant he realized that our two greatest fears about death are groundless. For what we fear most about death are the loss of our identity, and the end of meaningful existence. Those who see eternal life as a sort of anonymous merging into the cosmos give me no comfort. I want to know that my own personality—as undistinguished as it may seem to others—will continue after my death. It isn't enough for me to be a part of every tree and breeze and flower and sea spray. I want to be me, even as Mr. Smith did.

And in heaven he continues to be the same self-aware, conscious person that he has been since the moment of his birth. He is recognized and known in heaven, even as his loved ones and friends recognized and knew him here.

And as he needed a place in which to live here, so he has been given a place in heaven. Maybe not a wood or brick house with a certain address on a certain street, for these are earthly needs for our earthly style of life. But whatever kind of place he now needs has been prepared exclusively for him. He had been expecting that, really, having heard the words of Jesus: "I go to prepare a place for you" (Jn. 14:2). But that old promise has now become a present reality for him.

That new place of his is abundantly provided with everything he needs and wants. Exactly what those things are, I don't know. We tend to think of needs and wants as those things our bodies require—food, clothing, shelter. But I don't suppose Mr. Smith needs those things any more, any more than he needs his arthritis pain medicine or the bifocal glasses that he left on his bedside table in his old house.

But he does need love, as he needed it here; he needs acceptance; he needs the opportunity to do something meaningful; and he needs the confidence to face the future absolutely without fear. And he has all those things in perfect abundance.

And his treasure consists not only in what he now has, but also in what he knows he will never have again. As John put it in his description of heaven, "[God] will wipe every tear from their eyes. Death will be no more; mourning and crying and pain will be no more, for the first things have passed away."

Even as he is known and loved, so he knows and loves, for it is not enough to be loved; for life to be complete, we must have the opportunity to love. And not only has Mr. Smith found happy reunion with those whom he had loved before, he now finds it possible to love many others from whom the circumstances and limitations of this life had alienated him.

In the many years that my wife and I have been married, we have lived in many different houses. Some were rather large, some were quite small. We owned some of them and rented others. Some had several rooms, some only a few. But while I lived in each house, it was the most precious place on earth to me. Frequently I have driven many miles late at night, sometimes in difficult weather, to get back home to one of those houses. But I cannot now remember how many chairs there were in the living room of any of those residences, what color the walls were painted in the kitchen, or how the bedrooms were decorated. But at the time it was my home, it was precious to me, not because of where it was or what it was, but because of who was there.

So heaven is precious to Mr. Smith because of who is there. And more than loved ones and old friends are there. God is there, too. "See," John said in his description of heaven, "the home of God is among mortals. He will dwell with them as their God; they will be his peoples, and God himself will be with them." And in that presence, joy is complete.

Some time ago I faced an experience such as many others have also encountered, and perhaps you will recognize what I am about to describe. It was the day of my mother's funeral. Though her long illness had given me adequate time to prepare for the eventuality of her death, the stark reality of it was a shock to me nonetheless. And despite the fact that my work had frequently brought me into such experiences in the lives of other families, I steeled myself for her memorial service, knowing that it would be an emotional ordeal. Compounding the demands of the occasion were the usual complications that accrue to any unfamiliar experience: getting up very early in the morning and everyone—including several small children—getting dressed, finding clothing that would be suitable for the sad and formal occasion; driving a long distance; making last-minute arrangements that long-distance telephone calls had inadequately provided for; meeting friends and relatives from whom there had been long separation; worrying about remembering everyone's name.

Somehow the day passed, almost in a blur, and then there was another long trip by automobile to return to our son's home many miles distant. Finally, the day ended, we got out of the car, and my three-year-old grandson, Noah, remarked, to summarize the experience, "Haven't we had a wonderful day?" There was a shocked silence, none of the rest of the family knowing exactly what to say in answer to such an obviously inappropriate remark. But then it occurred to me that Noah was entirely right. It had been a wonderful day, filled with tenderness and consideration, and the love that expressed itself so beautifully in hugs and handshakes and flowers and food thoughtfully prepared and shared, and so many evidences of the human ties that are so often neglected or ignored when life whizzes by as it usually does. And underneath it all was the sudden realization that it was my mother's graduation day: After years of struggle and pain, she was free at last—released into the life eternal!

So Mr. Smith has gone to heaven. And for those of you who knew him, grieving for him is pointless, though you may indeed grieve for your own loneliness. But one day when death frees you from this temporary captivity, you will see Mr. Smith again, and perhaps he will meet you with the greeting, "What kept you so long?"

8

Chasing a Remembered Star

In the time of King Herod, after Jesus was born in Bethlehem of Judea, wise men from the East came to Jerusalem, asking, "Where is the child who has been born king of the Jews? For we have observed his star at its rising, and have come to pay him homage." When King Herod heard this, he was frightened, and all Jerusalem with him; and calling together all the chief priests and scribes of the people, he inquired of them where the Messiah was to be born. They told him, "In Bethlehem of Judea; for so it has been written by the prophet: 'And you, Bethlehem, in the land of Judah, are by no means least among the rules of Judah; for from you shall come a ruler who is to shepherd my people Israel.' Then Herod secretly called for the wise men and learned from them the exact time when the star had appeared. Then he sent them to Bethlehem, saying, "Go and search diligently for the child; and when you have found him, bring me word so that I may also go and pay him homage." When they had heard the king, they set out; and there, ahead of them, went the star that they had seen at its rising, until it stopped over the place where the child was. When they saw that the star had stopped, they were overwhelmed with joy. On entering the house, they saw the child with Mary his

mother; and they knelt down and paid him homage. Then,
opening their treasure chests, they offered him gifts of gold,
frankincense, and myrrh. (Mat. 2:1–11)

Butch Bender was the cross that had to be borne by my
Sunday school class. In those days, when children's classes were
divided into the smallest possible congruencies, there were three
boys who, year after year, constituted my class: Paul Johnson,
Wayne Love, and Bill Nichols. And none of us ever missed,
thanks in no small measure to three sets of parents who considered faithful attendance at Sunday school as much a part of a
child's armor against depravity as saying "Yes, ma'am," and "Yes,
sir," to adults and brushing after meals. Through summer heat
and winter cold, Paul, Wayne, and Bill manfully struggled through
the minor prophets and Paul's missionary journeys. Through
prosperous seasons of bumper attendance and through more
meager seasons, when the Sunday school superintendent pulled
at his chin and wondered aloud what this world was coming to,
the first-grade (or second-grade, or third- or fourth-) boys' class
maintained its record: Paul, Bill, and Wayne never missed.

About once a year, when the Sunday School Attendance
Contest was announced, the other classes would work over their
prospective member lists in the effort to increase their attendance sufficiently to merit bringing the Attendance Banner to
their classroom for the next week. It was always an unrewarding
time for my class, however, for Butch Bender constituted our
entire prospective member list. All the other boys our age were
either faithful attenders at another church or had clearly demonstrated their apathy—if not antipathy—to the whole idea of
Sunday school.

But Butch Bender was always an intriguing possibility, for
he had been known to attend our class on occasion, particularly
when treats were promised. A popcorn ball, an ice cream cone,
or a bag of candy would bring out Butch Bender the way spring
brought out the crocuses in the front yard. But these occasional

droppings-in seemed always to be strictly on Butch's own impulse and could never be prompted by all the urgings and pleadings of Bill, Wayne, or Paul. In fact, despite the unpredictable nature of his appearances, the one time we knew he would *not* be present was when we had begged him to come.

It was on Christmas Sunday when our threesome comprised the fourth-grade boys' class. Miss Naomi Flaherty, our teacher, had brought for each of us a colorfully wrapped present. All three boxes were identical in size, shape, and appearance, strongly suggesting the Sikorsky J-42 model airplane kit, which the three of us had discussed intensely the previous Sunday, at the expense of Daniel in the lions' den. Miss Flaherty was about ready to distribute the gifts when Butch Bender walked into the classroom. The color drained from the teacher's face. She had not expected him. In fact, she had never seen him, for she had been teaching the class only since October's Promotion Day.

The three of us—Paul, Wayne, and I—glared at Butch. We should have warned Miss Flaherty. Butch had pulled this trick before. But the teacher was clearly at a loss. Finally she asked Butch to take the offering envelope (to which Butch hadn't even contributed) to the superintendent's office. While he was gone, Miss Flaherty asked the three of us what we would suggest might be done. She pointed out that Butch did come from a very poor family, and that it was more his parents' fault than his own that he so seldom came to Sunday school. Just before Butch reentered the room, I heard myself saying through hot tears, "Give him mine."

Nobody offered any objection. Wayne and Paul looked the other way. Miss Flaherty was relieved. Butch was overjoyed. When they opened their gifts, each had a Sikorsky J-42 model airplane kit and I had nothing. Miss Flaherty whispered something that I did not hear, and the rest of the day—and for several days to come—I hated Butch Bender and cursed myself for being such a patsy.

Christmas came and went, and my resentment toward Butch was softened somewhat by the usual bounty of my Christmas emoluments. Then, on the first day back at school after our Christmas break, we went through the usual ritual of boasting about all our many gifts and proudly exhibiting those that we had brought to display. I had worn my new black leather gloves and had brought one wooden circle as evidence that I had received my own carom board set. Then I saw Butch, proudly showing off his Sikorsky J-42 model airplane. His talk all that day was of nothing but how he had carefully put it together and how much enjoyment he had received playing with it. Then suddenly the awful truth hit me: That had been Butch's only gift. Or, if not his only gift, certainly his best one.

My grudge began to melt and, despite the fact that I would still have enjoyed having my own Sikorsky J-42, I was almost glad he had it. I wanted to say something to Butch, but I couldn't think of anything to say. Nor did I know how to express what I felt to Miss Flaherty the next Sunday, or to my parents. I didn't even know exactly how I felt, except that it felt good somehow. And maybe that was the first time in my life I knew what Jesus meant when he said, "It is more blessed to give than to receive." And maybe, over the dark landscape of that childish disappointment, I saw a star.

How different life would be if only we could always keep sight of that star that directs us to behold God's truth! Unfortunately, however, we often go through long desert stretches when no star lifts up our eyes—or our hearts. And sometimes we find ourselves envying the wise men of the Christmas story, who were guided by that constant and compelling beacon in the sky, unerringly directing them—footstep by footstep—to the Christ child.

But if that is our picture of the wise men and their star, then we have missed something basic and highly significant in Matthew's account of that star-led journey. A careful reading of that story clearly indicates that most of the journey made by the wise men was done without the help and direction of the star. Matthew says that upon their arrival in Jerusalem, the wise men reported that they had seen the star at its rising—that is, they had glimpsed it at the beginning of its sky-borne journey. And impelled by that initial sign, they set out, not knowing where they were going, but following the direction indicated by that star as they remembered it. Apparently there had been no more recent sighting of it, from their Eastern homeland all the way to Jerusalem.

No wonder they stopped at Herod's palace, where the king's astrologers and sages would no doubt know of such a phenomenon, to inquire directions. But receiving no help, they continued that faith journey, chasing a remembered star, until when they left the city, the star appeared to them again. And the scripture reports that upon leaving Jerusalem, when they saw the star again, "they were overwhelmed with joy" (Mt. 2:10). Of course they were! It was the first clear sign they had received since leaving their homelands.

Talk about realism! Isn't that the way it happens with all of us? We all have our moments of seeing and knowing, when the star of understanding and certainty goes before us and we know that the road we are traveling is the right one. But then—nothing! Everything seems to go blank; the harsh realities of life intercede to diminish our vision; the busyness of day and the glare of the city lights at night conspire to blind us to the stars, and our journey of life loses its purpose and its joy.

But the wise men deserve their place in hallowed history not because they saw the star—for everybody sees a star sometimes—but because they had the courage to keep following the star when they could not see it. And because they did, they hold up before all of us a strategy by which life must be lived, if it is to fulfill its highest goals and discover its deepest peace.

One day you saw a star shining above your horizon that directed your feet toward your vocational choice—to be a minister, a homemaker, a nurse, a chemist, or a merchant, doctor, or teacher. How clearly you saw the heroic contributions you could make, the service you could render, the achievements you could attain! Then came the dreary landscape of daily demands and unrewarding drudgery, often without any word of thanks or any evidence that what you are doing is making any real difference in the world. How can you keep going when the star is lost?

One day you stood at the altar of God, holding the hand of one you promised to love, honor, and cherish, for better or worse, for richer or poorer, in sickness and in health. And there were stars in your eyes that day. But the day came—as it always does—when the stars got lost in an endless montage of alarm clocks, dirty dishes, pressing schedules, mortgage payments, and dripping faucets. How can you keep going when the star is lost?

One day you made your confession of faith in Jesus Christ, accepting him as Lord of your life. You followed a star that day, and you saw everything so clearly in its light. Righteousness would be your breastplate, salvation would be your helmet, and your days would be an endless psalm of praise. Then the world moved in on that dream, and dreary stretches of uninspiring—and sometimes faith-suffocating—disappointments made you wonder if you ever did see that star, or if it was only the invention of your gullible hope. Even for one as courageous and faithful as John the Baptist, it was hard to go on when he could not see the star. In the dungeon of Herod's persecution, John sent word to Jesus, whom he had once heralded as "the Lamb of God" (Jn. 1:29), to ask him plaintively, "Are you the one...or are we to wait for another?" (Mt. 11:2). How can we go on, when the star is lost?

The answer is in doing what the wise men so obviously did. Even when you can't see the star, you must remember and follow where it was leading the last time you could see it. It's like a child's puzzle of "connecting the dots" to make a picture. When you first see the puzzle, it seems to make no sense. But trace your pencil from one dot to another in order and something intelligible and beautiful emerges.

So with your life work: You can't always see the star of inspiration and challenge that you glimpsed at the beginning. But now and then it flickers slightly or shines brightly. And during those long stretches when the star is lost and inspiration fades, connect the dots of those times of clarity and purpose.

And when better or worse, richer or poorer, sickness or health becomes mostly worse, poorer, and sickness, remember those times when those stars in your eyes helped you to see clearly what joys and rewards would result from your faithfulness and commitment. And during those long stretches when the star is lost and inspiration fades, keep going in the direction you saw so clearly with those star-filled eyes.

And when your Christian discipleship seems to have gotten bogged down in the uninspiring day-to-day fulfilling of duties and the honoring of disciplines, remember those times when your vision was clear and your faith was validated by your experience, and connect the dots: Keep going in that direction.

I suppose the real point of the story of the wise men is that through their combination of vision—when they could see it— and courage—when they couldn't—they found Christ at the end of that journey. And that is enough of a point for me to keep looking for the stars of eternal truth and to keep going in the direction they showed me, even when I can't see them.

For as in all worthwhile pursuits, the road of Christian discipleship is frequently a matter of chasing a remembered star.

9
Ground Rules

*Then God spoke all these words: I am the LORD your
God, who brought you out of the land of Egypt, out of the
house of slavery; you shall have no other gods before me.
You shall not make for yourself an idol, whether in the form
of anything that is in heaven above, or that is on the earth
beneath, or that is in the water under the earth. You shall
not bow down to them or worship them; for I the LORD your
God am a jealous God, punishing children for the iniquity
of parents, to the third and the fourth generation of those
who reject me, but showing steadfast love to the thousandth
generation of those who love me and keep my commandments. You shall not make wrongful use of the name of the
LORD your God, for the LORD will not acquit anyone who
misuses his name. Remember the sabbath day, and keep it
holy. Six days you shall labor and do all your work. But the
seventh day is a sabbath to the LORD your God; you shall
not do any work—you, your son or your daughter, your
male or female slave, your livestock, or the alien resident in
your towns. For in six days the LORD made heaven and
earth, the sea and all that is in them, but rested the seventh
day; therefore the LORD blessed the sabbath day and consecrated*

it. Honor your father and your mother, so that your days may be long in the land that the LORD your God is giving you. You shall not murder. You shall not commit adultery. You shall not steal. You shall not bear false witness against your neighbor. You shall not covet your neighbor's house; you shall not covet your neighbor's wife, or male or female slave, or ox, or donkey, or anything that belongs to your neighbor. (Ex. 20:1–17)

After thirty-two years, I have decided to call it quits. Oh, there have been good times along the way, and week after week there has been much to enjoy and appreciate about this relationship, but there have been the bad times, too, and it just suddenly occurred to me that the bad has begun to outweigh the good and I have made up my mind to put an end to it. I'm canceling my subscription to *Time* magazine. Or, to be a bit more precise, I'm simply not renewing again, as I have done regularly every autumn since 1966. For thirty-two years I have faithfully subscribed and diligently read the weekly issues, even though at times I have not appreciated the definite editorial slant the writers have given their reporting of the news, and it has bothered me that every year the price seems to be increased. But finally, when that familiar mail-in subscription renewal form came again this year, I boldly checked the box beside the word "No," and sent it in without a check to cover my renewal.

I can only imagine what panic my reply brought to the head office of Time, Inc., in Chicago, when they received it. Surely high-level conferences were held and alarms were sounded. Strategists were assigned my case, and high-tech research facilities were tapped to try to understand my bizarre behavior. Why, after thirty-two years of faithfulness, was I suddenly behaving like a Benedict Arnold?

So the Department of Dire Consequences swung into action and initiated an intensive campaign to get me to retract my "No" and reconsider my cancellation. First a form letter came, suggesting condescendingly that I might have checked the wrong box in error and, before they did anything so extreme as to actually cancel my subscription, would I please reconfirm my reply by marking the enclosed reply card in the appropriate box. So I marked the "No" box again and sent it back.

Then, figuring, I suppose, that I must have been suffering from temporary insanity, they gave me a week or so to cool down and regain my composure, then they sent me a fresh, "let's-start-all-over-again" letter, asking that I think twice before actually going through with such an unthinkable course of action as my previous correspondence had indicated. Again, I returned the reply card with the "No" box clearly marked.

Next they began to trot out various inducements. Thinking I might be temporarily on my uppers financially, they suggested compassionately that I might take a full year to pay for the subscription in easy monthly installments. Again I answered "No." Then they thought they might sway me with the promise of gifts. How would I like a new Rand-McNally road atlas? How about a telephone with built-in calculator and night light? How about a three-volume pictorial history of World War II? Finally they began reducing their price. Would I like to continue receiving *Time* at the special educators' price? Or how about if they listed me with their licensed medical practitioners and gave me their special discount?

Then two weeks ago a young lady from the department, with a voice that strongly suggested that they had borrowed her from a television after-shave commercial, called to ask plaintively what was wrong, didn't I love them anymore?

And this week, when my positively, absolutely, definitely last issue of *Time* magazine arrived through the mail, it was contained in a special envelope with a personal hand-written message, calling me by name and warning me that the light was about to go out of my life.

And through all this, I have felt something of the frustration surely experienced by a rich playboy when he tries to divorce a

gold digger. And, to adapt a phrase that had political overtones
a while back, I have wanted to say to them, "Read my lips: no
new subscription!"

Why is it that some people find it so hard to believe that
there is sometimes in this world an absolute: a clearly drawn
line beyond which one will simply not go? I am offended by
Time magazine's apparent belief that my "No" can be changed
to "Yes" by a mail campaign, or a little soft soap, or a small
financial advantage, or the offer of a few trinkets. What has
happened to our integrity, when all our "Yes's" and all our "No's"
are for sale to the highest bidder?

I believe there are some things in this world that are right
and would be right under any circumstances, in any company,
no matter what arguments might be raised against them. And
conversely, I believe that there are some things that are wrong,
in and of themselves, and they would be wrong in any circumstances, in any company, and no matter what inducements or
advantages might be offered as justification for doing them. I
believe there is such a thing as truth in this universe—dependable,
eternally unwavering truth—and its preeminence and permanence do not depend upon how popular it happens to be at the
moment.

Several years ago, Ernest Campbell, former minister of Riverside Church in New York, wrote a book that he called *No Fault
Morality.* An avid golfer, he suggests that what has happened to
morality in America is like what happened to him when he was
learning the game of golf. He didn't take up the game until he
was pastor of Riverside Church and some of his deacons thought
it would do him good and improve his state of mind if he went
out once or twice a week to play golf. So they undertook to
teach him the game. And though they were championship golf-
ers, they were very kind and nonjudgmental toward their pastor, as he flubbed his way through his first few rounds. When he
topped the ball on the first tee, leaving the ball in its original
position, they would say, "Ernie, that's all right. We won't count

it. Let's call it a mulligan. Hit it again." Only when he hit the ball a reasonable distance would they make him count it. And on the greens, if his ball was fifteen feet from the cup and theirs were only inches from the cup, they would say charitably, "Ernie, it's a gimme! We'll give you yours, if you'll give us ours."

So Ernest Campbell got to be within his own circle a fair golfer, never realizing how much he was depending upon bending the rules, until he played in a public tournament and found, to his humiliation, how inflexible the rules of golf really were and how stubbornly unmoving the other players could be when he expected to be exempt from a strict obedience to the rules.

And I have an uncomfortable feeling that all over America, thousands of people today are taking "mulligans" and "gimmes" all over the place and think they are playing by the rules of life. They decide for themselves as they go along which rules they will obey and which they will set aside, if there is sufficient justification in their own minds for doing so. But they are living in a fool's paradise, and one day they will come into some situation in which it will be revealed to them in some unforgettable way: There is an absolute standard of truth at the center of life, and nothing that opposes it—for any reason—will survive, and nothing that upholds it—in any circumstances—will be defeated.

After leading the Hebrew people out of their time of slavery in Egypt, Moses had on his hands an unruly, undisciplined, disorganized rabble of several hundred thousand fugitives from justice. Having just escaped from strict authority, they were rebellious, contentious, unprincipled, and impossible to organize. Moses realized that if they were not to die in the wilderness from internecine struggles, their dream of the promised land unrealized, they would have to be unified somehow, into a working team, focused by a single high purpose, and governed by a single code of dependable laws by which they would all live together harmoniously.

So three months after they had crossed the Red Sea to leave their Egyptian bondage, Moses went up into the height of Mount

Sinai and received from God the Law—the Ten Commandments. The natural assumption of the humanists is that Moses himself was the author of these laws. If that were the case, then Moses was certainly the wisest and most farsighted man who ever lived, because the ten simple statements he brought down from the mountain (in most of the commandments, a single word in the original Hebrew) are the most concise and at the same time the most comprehensive statements of the basic laws of human conduct in society ever formulated. For thousands of years, they have been the basis for living together in harmony in this world. And in every nation in the Western world, including the United States of America, those Ten Commandments have provided the basic foundation stone upon which all our other laws are based.

But the story in Exodus confidently asserts that these were not the laws of Moses, but the laws of God. And in giving us these laws for life, God shows us that life is meant to be lived in a certain way, within certain perimeters. And the purpose of the laws is not to deny us freedom, but to show us how life may be lived to achieve the greatest success and happiness and to make the greatest contribution to our world. There are rules in every game, and those rules are simply instructions telling how to play the game and how to win. Rules are not meant to break our spirits, but to instruct and focus our efforts so as to achieve what we really want.

And since it was God who created life, God had a right to tell us how that life was to be lived. And here is what God said:

> You shall have no other gods before me.
> You shall not make for yourself an idol…
> You shall not make wrongful use of the name of the
>   LORD your God…
> Remember the sabbath day, and keep it holy…
> Honor your father and your mother…
> You shall not murder.

You shall not commit adultery.

You shall not steal.

You shall not bear false witness against your neighbor.

You shall not covet. (Ex. 20:1–17)

Or, to summarize it in an even smaller capsule, God was saying that the only way to live successfully in this life is to live in such a way as to show reverence to God and respect to each other and to ourselves. That's it—that's all. And, as Jesus was to say, many centuries later, "Do this, and you will live" (Lk. 10:28).

The people of Israel responded to the first reading of this law in a very strange way. When Moses finished the reading of it, they said to him, "All that the LORD has spoken, we will do and we will be obedient." (Ex. 24:7). Do you hear that? Theirs was not faith that resulted in obedience, but obedience that resulted in faith. They didn't yet have the faith that Moses had, or the faith that they would themselves have one day. But they were smart enough to realize that there was an authority in life, and they were wise enough to recognize that they must accept and respect that authority and show it by adhering to the laws that represented the truth established by that authority.

When our children were small, their mother and I tried diligently to reason with them, in helping them to adopt habits and behaviors that would be beneficial to them. But sometimes they simply did not want to brush their teeth, take a bath, or go to bed early. And since they demonstrated an astonishing verbal ability at a very young age and since they knew we wanted to be reasonable with them, they frequently contested our directions. Ordinarily their rebuttals would begin with the question, "Why?" Why do I have to take a bath? Why do I have to go to bed? After we had exhausted our patience, there was one last "explanation" that frequently ended the discussion: "Because we're bigger than you are and it's our house." Undemocratic? Of course, but it was important for them to discover that in life there is authority that must be accepted and obeyed.

And there is an authority in all life. Whether we agree with it or not, whether we like it or not, that authority must be acknowledged and obeyed. And in this house of life, that authority is God. God is bigger than we are and it's God's house. And until we accept the authority of God and are willing to make peace with the truth that God has put into life as the basis for all human conduct, we shall never find real peace. "In his will," Augustine rightly said, "is our peace."

10
The Key to Judging

"Do not judge, so that you may not be judged. For with the judgment you make you will be judged, and the measure you give will be the measure you get. Why do you see the speck in your neighbor's eye, but do not notice the log in your own eye? Or how can you say to your neighbor, 'Let me take the speck out of your eye,' while the log is in your own eye? You hypocrite, first take the log out of your own eye, and then you will see clearly to take the speck out of your neighbor's eye." (Mt. 7:1−5)

A few years ago I realized a long-standing dream of mine when one Sunday afternoon at Camden, Maine, I boarded the sailing ship "The Adventure" and began a six-day experience of sailing the North Atlantic. I had long fantasized about what a wonderful experience that would be on the slanting deck of a handsome schooner, with acres of white canvas above me catching the ocean breezes, with nothing but clear sky above and nothing but the mysterious depths of ocean beneath. I would be another Magellan, fixing my steely eyes on some dimly envisioned harbor beyond the uncharted seas, letting the salt spray wash my face and the fierce winds play in my uncombed hair, as I sang with my shipmates the old sea chanteys like "Sixteen men on a dead man's chest, yo ho ho and a bottle of Diet Rite Cola!" That was the dream!

But the colorful brochures that lured me to sign up for that adventure failed to mention certain details that I soon discovered on my own. Somehow in all my fantasies I had never come to grips with the necessity of shaving in cold salt water every morning; having neither a shower nor a bathtub on board; having no chair of any kind to sit in for six days; having no shelter from the torrential rains for which the North Atlantic is notorious; the unmitigated labor of hoisting an anchor that weighs only about a ton, unless you are the one who is hoisting it, when it suddenly becomes more like a hundred tons; the temperatures, which range from torrid when you are unprotected from the midday sun, to frigid when the sun goes down; or the rope burns and calluses and sunburn, which are the most tangible souvenirs of such an adventure.

No, nobody told me about those things. But now that I know such things are inescapable facts of sailing on the ocean, what would I do if I were invited to take another such trip? I would say, "Just give me five minutes to change my clothes!"

I believe that all of life's greatest joys are found not in ideal, flawless situations, but in discovering and savoring the glory in any situation that flaws cannot diminish and imperfections cannot destroy—*unless we let them.*

Sometimes people are attracted to Jesus and his teachings because they believe he lived an idyllic life and lifted up before us the prospects of an untroubled existence that is free from difficulties and frustrations. But the gospel is really a complicated story of a young man from Nazareth who knew all the same frustrations and difficulties and temptations that any young man knows and who worked hard—first as a carpenter, then as an itinerant preacher—and who enjoyed precious little success and experienced many discouragements and who was finally killed by his enemies.

The biblical story of Jesus' life withholds no grimy detail of his experiences. You can almost smell the cattle stall in which he was born and the dirty, sweaty feet he washed in the upper room; the dust of the roads he traveled can almost be felt in our throats. You identify with his struggles to pay taxes and to find food to feed people whose hunger pushed their manners to the edge of irritability. You can understand his courageous attempts to remain patient with the stubbornly obtuse and openly hostile. There are enough blood, toil, sweat, and tears in Jesus' life story to provide grist for the mills of a dozen soap operas. Nevertheless, toward the end of that short life, Jesus, even on the eve of his execution, said calmly to his followers, "I have said these things to you so that my joy may be in you, and that your joy may be complete" (Jn. 15:11).

And if you choose to follow Jesus, you must be warned by the words of the apostle Peter, who wrote, "Christ also suffered for you, leaving you an example, so that you should follow in his steps" (1 Pet. 2:21). And following in those steps, you will probably not find any serene, untroubled Elysian Fields, where you may lie down in unruffled relaxation. As his follower, you will find life as full of frustrations, flaws, and hazards as he found it, but you will also find the glory and the joy that made him love this world enough to die for it.

It is well for us to remember that Jesus' challenge to his disciples—now as then—is not "Are you willing?" but "Are you able?" (Mt. 20:22). Although a willing spirit is a prerequisite for the follower of Jesus, it must be clearly understood that a life of Christian discipleship is not for the comfort-seeker.

In his Sermon on the Mount, Jesus sought to give to his followers a master key to living happily, abundantly, and victoriously in this world. And he could certainly not accomplish that unless he helped us accept and deal with the imperfections and flaws in the world around us and in the lives of the people with whom we must share this world.

In one of his most striking illustrations, he said, "Why do you see the speck in your neighbor's eye, but do not notice the log in your own eye?" This little gem of an illustration is a splendid example of the kind of teaching that made Jesus' addresses so enjoyable to his audiences. It was intended, of course, as humor. It was a ridiculous hyperbole, an outrageous exaggeration. Jesus was very good at that sort of thing and, though nowhere in the gospel stories are we told that the multitudes roared with laughter at his little stories, I believe that it is a justifiable conclusion for us to draw. He once spoke of the nit-picking Pharisees fastidiously straining a gnat that had fallen into their cup, but failing to notice a whole camel that had somehow fallen into that same cup and gulping it down—hair, humps, hoofs, and all. Oh, I suspect the people laughed at that, all right. But they got the point that Jesus intended: It is ridiculous to spend all your time and effort trying to deal with things of minor importance, while letting matters of great, eternal significance go unheeded.

So, in this little teaching about the speck and the log, he was making an important statement in a humorous and memorable way. Think of the contrast between a speck and a log! The word translated here as "speck," and in the King James version as "mote," referred to those tiny particles that you see swimming in a shaft of bright sunlight. I don't know what they are—dust, maybe: tiny bits of matter so small you cannot see them at all, unless you have a strong light or view them through a microscope. Then here is the contrasting object: a log—a huge tree cut down to serve as a girder to support a house or a roof. Now imagine this ridiculous picture: A person, who—quite unconscious of his own enormous problem of having a beam stuck in his eye—is bothered by the sight of another person who has the tiniest speck of dust in his eye, and says condescendingly, "I see you have this speck in your eye. Here, your poor thing, let me help you get it out."

Now the first important inference to be drawn from this teaching is that there are specks in life everywhere. This is a speckled world, and if you go looking for specks you will surely see them, in everything and in everybody. To see the specks in other people proves only that you are reasonably intelligent. But to see only the specks proves that you are unreasonably critical and uncompassionate.

Of course, there are specks of imperfection in your marriage, in your work situation, in your city, your church, your school. But while there is much that is wrong, there may also be very much that is right. And when we spend so much of our time being critical and cynical, we are denying others the understanding and compassion that, as children of God, they deserve, and we are denying ourselves the glory and the joy of life that accrue only to those who are able to accept the specks as part of the real world in which we live, without letting them destroy that world for us.

"Why do you see the speck?" Jesus asked. Why do you keep your attention focused upon the little that is bad when there is so very much that is good? You see, it is my conviction that, as Christians, we have no right to be cynical. It shows a lack of gratitude to God for the much that is magnificently good about life and in the lives of people around us; furthermore, it serves only to draw attention to the imperfections in our own lives.

A most proper lady once went to call upon her next-door neighbors, parents of two boys, to complain to them that their sons insisted upon singing vulgar and obscene songs within her hearing. The parents were shocked. "Are you sure?" they asked. "We have never heard them singing any such songs. In fact, they are not much given to singing at all. And we don't know where they could have learned such songs. Are you sure they were singing vulgar and obscene songs?" "Well," the woman replied in a huff, "they may not have been singing them, but I definitely heard them *humming* them."

But whom did her complaint really indict? Such an accusation reminds us that when we point a finger of accusation at anyone else, we are pointing one finger at them, but at the same time pointing three fingers back at ourselves. It is a strange quirk of human nature that we are quickest to detect in others those sins of which we ourselves are guilty. And though one would think we would be the most understanding of those whose sins are most like ours, those are the people of whom we are the most judgmental. Psychologists have pointed out that it may be our own guilt that we are trying to punish when we lash out in judgment against those whose sins resemble ours.

So Jesus formulated this frightening rule of life: "With the judgment you make you will be judged, and the measure you give will be the measure you get." The most critical will be the most criticized, but the most forgiving will be the most forgiven. Who of us then can afford to be critical and unforgiving? Who of us is so without sin that we can justify casting the first stone?

In the "Peanuts" comic strip, Charlie Brown and his cynical friend Lucy were having a profound discussion one day about the world. Lucy asks, "Charlie Brown, why are some people good and other people bad?" And Charlie Brown answers with a question, "Who is to say? Who is to say who is good and who is bad?" Lucy answers eagerly, "I will!" And there are many people like Lucy, who are so very willing and so very prompt to decide who is good and who is bad. But Jesus emphasizes that we have no right to make such judgments.

The Native Americans used to say that you should not judge your neighbor until you have walked a whole day in his moccasins. You see, we simply do not know enough about other people's lives to know what makes them do what they do. I have never been tempted to be an alcoholic. It is absolutely no struggle for me. But I cannot be harsh in my judgment of alcoholics, because I have never been faced with their battle; though they lose those battles now and again, I know that much of the time they struggle against that temptation with heroic strength that would beggar many of my struggles against temptation.

Karl Barth, the theologian, said that we have no right to judge others because the dividing line is always hidden from us. But despite the clear prohibition of Jesus and the teachings of the saints and the wisdom of our own common sense, one of the most characteristic marks of many Christian groups is the absoluteness of their judgments that those who disagree with their doctrines are ipso facto wrong. Only God can be that sure, and we have it on the authority of holy scripture that God is more understanding and more ready to forgive than we are.

But as Christians we must make some response to flaws in the world around us. Jesus was not blind to sin and injustice, nor does he ask us to be. Rather he asks us to be humble and helpful in approaching the sins of others. First, recognize that you, too, are a sinner. And if you are not as guilty as the person you are trying to help, it may be only because of one of two reasons: Either you have not suffered the same temptations in the same degree or you have been forgiven of your sins. In either case, you have no reason to be arrogant. Paul said, "My friends, if anyone is detected in a transgression, you who have received the Spirit should restore such a one in a spirit of gentleness. Take care that you yourselves are not tempted" (Gal. 6:1). Remember who and what you are, and remember that your only justifiable response to one who has failed should be a gentle and loving effort to restore, to help that person find another chance.

In a small community there was an old derelict named Tom, who was forever the butt of the cruel jokes and ridicule of all who knew him. One day the minister happened along, just in time to see a group of schoolboys throwing rocks at him and calling him names. The minister made the boys stop and, when they had all gone away, the derelict asked, "Pastor, why do you suppose people mistreat me so?" The minister, thinking perhaps he could make a lesson out of the experience, replied, "Well, Tom, maybe they are doing it to make you improve." And the old man replied, "I don't remember hearing of your Jesus throwing rocks at anyone to make them improve."

And, come to think of it, neither do I. When people responded to Jesus, it was because he loved them as no one else ever had and looked hard enough to find the good in them that nobody else had ever looked hard enough to find, encouraged it and rejoiced in it.

That is a spirit that the world desperately needs now, for there is a lot of bitterness, a lot of hatred, and a lot of suspicion in our time. No matter how well we know the Bible, no matter how intelligently we may be able to argue theology, no matter how sacrificially we may serve the church, what the world really needs from Christians today is that loving spirit that forgives the bad and that encourages, calls forth, believes in, and appreciates the good in ordinary folk.

And that was Jesus' key to judging.

11

Remembered Words, Forgotten Music

Beloved, while eagerly preparing to write you about the salvation we share, I find it necessary to write and appeal to you to contend for the faith that was once for all entrusted to the saints. (Jude 3)

Wake up, and strengthen what remains and is on the point of death, for I have not found your works perfect in the sight of my God. Remember then what you received and heard; obey it, and repent. (Rev. 3:2–3)

The three pint-sized salesmen at my front door had given me their best sales pitch to persuade me to buy whatever it was they were selling, to support whatever school or band or scout troop whose coffers they were seeking to fill by their commercial efforts. Being known far and wide as an easy mark for such amateur merchandising efforts, I had succumbed and was now emptying my billfold and various and sundry pockets in order to accumulate the total amount to which I had obligated myself. In counting out the assortment of bills and coins into the young hand outstretched to me, I inadvertently dropped a penny and crouched down on the front porch to retrieve it.

I could tell that such a small prize hardly tempted any search-and-rescue effort on the part of the three youngsters. And I suppose a penny doesn't mean much to young people who cannot remember when a package of chewing gum cost less than thirty cents. So they simply stood there and allowed me to search. When at last I retrieved the penny, I sought to justify my effort by saying, "Many mickles make a muckle." The three young faces looked at my blankly. One asked, "What's a mickle?" The second inquired, "What's a muckle?" And the third, though not saying anything, was clearly wondering, "What's the difference?"

That experience has led me in the past few days to ask myself what has happened to all the proverbs and maxims that were in such common currency when I was growing up. As I reflect upon it, I believe my mother presided over my growing up, armed with a bottomless supply of such proverbs that represented the accumulated wisdom of many generations. By the time I was ten, I had learned all my mother's maxims by heart and could see them coming a mile away. Asking to stay up past my normal bedtime, I knew that her denial of my request would be explained with, "Early to bed, early to rise, makes a man healthy, wealthy, and wise." If I whimpered about having to get up early in the morning, I could depend on her to say, "The early bird gets the worm." If I besought her for a sweet treat after school, I knew that she would steer me toward a more sensible choice of fruit with her admonition, "An apple a day keeps the doctor away."

The one I most despised was, "If at first you don't succeed, try, try again." This was the battle cry with which she constantly sent me back into every hopeless struggle and unpromising effort that I would have preferred to abandon after a single fruitless effort.

I soon discovered that my mother was not the sole possessor of such wisdom. Every adult that populated my childhood years seemed to know exactly when was the right time for such a warning as, "The devil finds work for idle hands to do." If I interrupted an adult conversation, every adult present competed for the right to be the first to say, "Children are meant to be seen and not heard." And if I only sat quietly listening to an adult conversation that veered toward the scandalous, one of the grown-ups present was sure to cast a surreptitious glance in my direction and warn, "Little pitchers have big ears."

In thinking about this matter, it has occurred to me that my mother came along at the tail-end of the last generation that learned to read from the old McGuffey Readers, in which the acquisition of reading skills was coupled with the propagation of moral truths. Instead of "Run, Spot, Run," fledgling readers were given proverbs that distilled the wisdom of many generations in matters of morals and manners. By the time a student had copied the sentence "A penny saved is a penny earned " fifty times in his copy book, he had not only improved his penmanship but had also absorbed an important truth about thrift.

More recent generations have found replacements for the old axioms. We now have bumper stickers like "If it feels good, do it" and television commercial jingles like "Grab all the gusto you can get." The other day I heard a youngster say, as he and his mother headed for the family car, "Looks like a Stroh's Light night."

I wonder if there is any significance in the fact that the Christian Church (Disciples of Christ) spent its childhood and youth in the McGuffey Reader years. The growing up of our church was also guided by proverbs and axioms, slogans and epigrams that no member of the church in those days could avoid learning, any more than I could have avoided learning that "fools' names and fools' faces (are) often seen in public places." Though the early theologians of the Christian Church (Disciples of Christ) were men of great erudition, their words, which fired the multitudes and swept across frontier America like a brush fire, were simply worded slogans that even children in Sunday school could understand and remember.

And seldom in history has a new religious movement enjoyed such an astonishing spread and growth as the Disciples of Christ in the nineteenth century. Within a half century of its founding, the Christian Church had built numerous colleges and universities, had planted congregations from coast to coast and border to border, had clearly demonstrated a national leadership in ecumenical affairs, and had produced major scholars and a host of distinguished statesmen, educators, and artists (like James A. Garfield, president of the United States; Michael Faraday, scientist; and Vachel Lindsay, poet).

The membership of the Christian Church increased at such a phenomenal rate in its first fifty years that if our present constituency were to continue to grow at that rate, in less than a decade from now, every man, woman, youth, and child in the United States would be added to our membership rolls.

And the marching music that gave spirit and zeal to the Christian Church in its early days was the slogans and axioms. Surely nowhere in the world was there a group of Disciples of Christ who could not quote those theological maxims.

And though we still know them, somehow the music has gone out of them. Mark Twain's wife once tried to cure her husband of violent swearing by repeating verbatim a long stream of curses he had just let fly. Twain looked at his wife condescendingly and said, "Honey, you know the words, but you just don't know the tune." In a sense, I suspect, that is true of us. If pressed, most of us could at least fill in the blanks to complete the slogans of nineteenth-century Discipledom, but the thrill is gone. They don't set our hearts to singing or our feet to marching. We remember the words; we have forgotten the music.

The first of these slogans was this: "Where the scriptures speak, we speak; where the scriptures are silent, we are silent." It was Thomas Campbell who coined that slogan in 1809, to provide some basis and some authority for transcending the bitter disputes and hostilities that had sundered the church. And that slogan became the rallying cry for those who were tired of the tyranny of human opinions and the resulting trivialization of matters of eternal concern. In Campbell's first American pastorate, a Presbyterian church in Western Pennsylvania, he found the elders of the church refusing to serve communion to those whose opinions on matters of municipal policy in Scotland differed from their own. It was Campbell's conviction that when we allow human opinion to rule in the church, divine intention suffers. So he called his followers to be guided by the slogan, "Where the scriptures speak, we speak; where the scriptures are silent, we are silent."

And that was the marching song that impelled the Disciples to victory after victory, as they focused their minds and their work and their witness upon the great central truths of the Christian faith, speaking forcefully and vigorously on behalf of those truths, but remaining silent on matters not specifically directed by inspired scripture. That led to another slogan: "In essentials, unity; in non-essentials, liberty; in all things, charity." While other denominational groups argued and divided and split, the Disciples prospered with the formula that called for faithful adherence to those things specifically spelled out in scripture, liberty in matters of opinion about which sincere Christians might have honest differences, but with a brotherly and sisterly love that undergirded all things in the church. No wonder the church grew!

But while we remember the words, we seem to have forgotten the music. Those words no longer set our hearts to singing or our feet to marching. And that's too bad, because the formula the Disciples offered the world in its beginning is a formula needed even more badly today. The world still hungers—starves—to hear the word of God proclaimed boldly, accurately, confidently, unequivocally. And we cannot pick and choose from the Bible's messages, requiring strict adherence only to those tenets that appeal to us and ignoring the rest. When the Bible calls for faith in Jesus Christ, we must accept that and proclaim that. But when the Bible calls us to the more difficult matters of racial and economic justice and world peace and the elimination of hunger and disease and poverty, we cannot pretend that we have not heard that message. Where the Bible speaks, we dare not be silent.

Another slogan that provided the marching music for the Disciples in the early days was this: "We are not the only Christians; we are Christians only." When the earliest Disciples chose the simple name "Christian" for our church, they were saying not that they thought themselves to be the only true Christians, but that they felt that being a Christian was important enough in itself not to have to limit it by any party label or denominational modifier. They extended their arms warmly to *Catholic* Christians, to *Baptist* Christians, and to *Moravian* and *Methodist* Christians, preferring to think of them as Catholic *Christians,* Baptist *Christians,* Moravian or Methodist *Christians, or,* better yet, as Christians only.

This was the song that provided the harmony that had been tragically lacking in the music of the church. And that harmony is still urgently needed, but though we remember the words, we seem to have forgotten the music. Indeed, for many of us, having such a transparent name for our church as "Christian" often seems only an inconvenience and an embarrassment akin to having no name at all. But as we have been slowly learning, the nouns tend to unite; the adjectives tend to separate and divide. Adjectives like black and white, rich and poor, Democrat and Republican, conservative and liberal—they're all fighting words! But when we can see that black or white, rich or poor, a man's a man, a woman's a woman, then we have united on the noun instead of being divided by the adjective.

So, conservative or liberal, high-church or low-church, evangelical or ecumenical, a Christian's a Christian and should be regarded as such by other Christians. What Christ has united by his redemptive love should not be sundered by anyone's exclusiveness.

A final slogan of early-day Discipledom was this: "The church of Christ is essentially, intentionally, and constitutionally one church." This statement from Campbell's "Declaration and Address" meant to convey that Christ's church on earth was meant by its founder, Jesus Christ, to be one, and that despite all our human efforts to splinter it, the church remains essentially one, and that we'd better recognize that and accept it. That means that Saint Francis of Assisi doesn't just belong to the Catholics, but to all Christians everywhere. He belongs to our church. And so do Martin Luther and Martin Luther King, Jr., and John Calvin, and Billy Graham and Norman Vincent Peale and Mother Theresa and John Wesley and Albert Schweitzer. Not *my* church, nor *their* church, not even *our* church, but *Christ's* church. The early Disciples found the wealth of their faith multiplied by opening the doors of fellowship to include those who had been Catholics and Baptists, Presbyterians and Congregationalists. Every congregation was a melting pot of religious tradition and religious and political opinion. And there was joy in both the unity and in the diversity. That joy was the music of the church.

It was in that spirit that one of the Disciples' early poets, Edwin Markham, wrote:

He drew a circle that left me out—
  Heretic, rebel, a thing to flout.
But love and I had a wit to win:
  We drew a circle that took him in.

And from our earliest days, the Christian Church (Disciples of Christ) has been in the business of tearing down walls and building bridges, drawing circles of inclusion as wide as the heart of God, in order that our Lord's prayer for his followers might be fulfilled: "that they may be one" (Jn. 17:11).

These were the slogans that brought a song to our hearts and set our feet to marching. And we've remembered the words, but forgotten the music.

During the Civil War, a young soldier became sick on the battlefield and was taken to the hospital tent behind the lines.

Lying there on a cot, he pleaded with the doctor, "Oh, doctor, don't tell me I'm not fit for duty. Don't tell me I can't go back to the front again. It's only a touch of the fever, Doc, and the sound of the bugle will make me well again!"

And that is my undying hope for the church. Our church has been—and is—subject to a wide range of debilitating ailments and weaknesses. But can't you hear the bugle call—the sound of the trumpet calling us to recover our holy purpose? That is what the whole world is listening for: a lifting up of a clear and positive blast on the trumpet of the living God. And I pray that the sound of that bugle will make the church well again, as we remember the words and the *music* that will put a song in our hearts and set our feet to marching again!

12

"In Remembrance of Me"...Embrace One Another

*From now on, therefore, we regard no one from a human
point of view; even though we once knew Christ from a human point of view, we know him no longer in that way. So
if anyone is in Christ, there is a new creation: everything
old has passed away; see, everything has become new! All
this is from God, who reconciled us to himself through Christ,
and has given us the ministry of reconciliation; that is, in
Christ God was reconciling the world to himself, not counting their trespasses against them, and entrusting the message of reconciliation to us. So we are ambassadors for
Christ, since God is making his appeal through us; we en-
treat you on behalf of Christ, be reconciled to God. (2 Cor.
5:16–20)*

During the Middle Ages there was, according to legend, a
time of discord in Jerusalem. At that time, the Holy City was
controlled by Christians, who appealed to the pope in Rome,

This is an abridged version of an address delivered at the Sunday evening
session of the General Assembly of the Christian Church (Disciples of Christ),
in Tulsa in October 1991.

asking him to use his power to banish all Jews from Jerusalem. In answer to this request, the pope decided to go to Jerusalem, to hold a kind of summit meeting with the chief rabbi, the highest Jewish authority. As with many confrontations between parties with differing points of view, the meeting soon became a debate, which would decide the fate of the Jews. If the pope won, the Jews would have to leave the city. If the Chief Rabbi won, the Jews could stay.

They met in a cathedral in Jerusalem. The two great men were seated in large chairs facing each other—the pope in his splendid robes, surrounded by cardinals and bishops, the chief rabbi robed and surrounded by advisers and counselors. Each side was allowed to set one condition on the debate. The pope said that since neither could speak or understand the other's language anyway, the debate should be done only in gestures and symbols—without any words being spoken. The chief rabbi stipulated that it should be done without an audience. So everyone else left, leaving the two leaders facing each other.

The pope began the debate by sweeping his hand in a great arc. The chief rabbi responded by pointing to the floor. The pope then held up three fingers. The chief rabbi responded by holding up one finger. The pope reached over to the sideboard and lifted a chalice of wine. The chief rabbi removed from under his robes an apple and held it up. The pope threw up his hands, crying, "That's enough! You've won! What a brilliant argument! Your theology is impeccable. The Jews may remain in Jerusalem."

The doors were thrown open and everyone rushed into the hall. The pope and the chief rabbi were swept to opposite sides of the room. The cardinals rushed up to the pope and asked, "What happened? How did the chief rabbi win the argument?" The pope said, "He was magnificent. I said, by my gesture, 'God is everywhere.' He said, by his gesture, 'Yes, but God is right here, too.' I said, 'But God is here in three persons: Father, *Son*, and Holy Spirit.' He said, 'Yes, but there is still only one God.' I held up the chalice of wine to say, 'But we Christians are saved by the shed blood of Jesus Christ.' He held up an apple to say, 'But as with Adam, all of us have sinned, and have fallen short of the glory of God, thus we are all equal in the sight of God.' I admitted that this was brilliant. He had won. I had nothing more to say."

Across the room the chief rabbi was asked by his advisers, "What happened? How did you win?" "I'm not sure," he responded. "The pope said, by his gestures, 'All you Jews must leave Jerusalem.' I said, by my gesture, 'We're staying right here.' He said, 'You have three days to leave town.' I said, 'Not one Jew is leaving.' Then he stopped the debate and reached for some wine to take with his lunch. So I took out an apple that I had been saving for my lunch, and that's when he threw up his hands and declared that I had won!"

I must confess to a great fondness for that story for many reasons. For one thing it demonstrates how easily our words and gestures may distort, rather than report, what we really feel and want to say. But beyond that, the story illustrates how one's religious faith and spirit speak a language of their own, sometimes achieving a unity that might forever elude the letter and the logic. And I love those symbols: the apple and the chalice—the apple reminding us of our sin and weakness and rebellion, which have resulted in the fragmentation of our own lives and our society, and the chalice, symbolizing the only means by which our human and societal brokenness might be healed. As Paul's magnificent declaration said it in his Ephesian epistle, "But now in Christ Jesus you who once were far off have been brought near by the blood of Christ. For he is our peace; in his flesh he has made both groups into one and has broken down the dividing wall, that is, the hostility between us" (Eph. 2:13–14).

Unfortunately, this is a world that knows its apples far better than it knows his chalice. The brokenness of our world is painfully demonstrated in every arena of human interaction: war among nations, internecine struggles within nations, racial and ethnic rivalries, sectarian violence, neighborhood feuds. Who is speaking for Christ these days? Who is bringing the peace of Christ's redemptive acceptance and love to the brokenness of the world?

Tragically, though the church has been divinely assigned this glorious ministry, we ourselves have allowed the bitterness of division and hostility to fragment the family of God. We deserve the cynicism of a world that is skeptical of our efforts to promote peace in the world and among its peoples, saying to the church, "Physician, heal thyself." And we deserve the bitter rebuke of the Christ, as he points to his church and says to us, "This is *my* body, broken *by* you."

And how many are the individuals whose broken lives need the redemptive love that Christ has given us to share? Why are we so stingy with that healing love? How carefully we scrutinize the credentials of those whom we might favor by accepting them into our Christian family bond! How tediously we scan their qualifications, and how quick we are to conclude that some do not deserve the love of Christ that would make them part of our church! And how swift is our judgment on those whose opinions differ from ours or whose lifestyle does not conform to ours.

I am haunted by a little poem that Emily Dickinson wrote. Count me as among those who have been lifted to heaven by the inspiration of her verse. She spoke for God. And yet, during her lifetime she was rejected by Christians, excluded by the church because she was a misfit, one whose marching to a different drum made her a scandal to the lockstepping drum corps of the society in which she lived. Most of the time she kept the hurt of her rejection to herself. But in one of her compositions she poured out her heart:

> Why—do they shut me out of Heaven?
> Did I sing—too loud?
> But—I can say a little "Minor"
> Timid as a Bird!

Wouldn't the Angels try me—
Just—once—more—
Just—see—if I troubled them—
But don't—shut the door!

Oh, if I—were the Gentleman
In the "White Robe"—
And they—were the little Hand—that knocked—
Could I forbid?

Well, could you? Do you? By your judgment, your withholding of acceptance and understanding to those whom your Christ loved enough to die for, are you shutting them out of heaven?

Let us understand perfectly well, Christians, that of all the gifts and obligations Christ lavished upon his church, judgment is not one of them. Closing the gate of heaven in the faces of those whose convictions differ from ours is not one of them! Rather, listen to what Paul says has been given the church as its raison d'etre: "All this is from God, who reconciled us to himself through Christ, and has given us the ministry of reconciliation."

And to accomplish this magnificent and sorely needed ministry in the world, we have only one instrument: the astonishing love of Jesus Christ, who reached out to embrace us even when we were totally unworthy of it and which then reaches out through us to those no more deserving of it than we are. And it is only when that love is totally undeserved that it is really love. As Jesus pointed out in his Sermon on the Mount, "If you love those who love you, what reward do you have? Do not even the tax collectors do the same? And if you greet only your brothers and sisters, what more are you doing than others? Do not even the Gentiles do the same?" (Mt. 5:46–47).

You may remember the powerful play *A Raisin in the Sun*, by Lorraine Hansberry. It tells the story of a poor black family from Chicago's south side. After the father's death, the mother wants to use his insurance money to move her family into a little house on the other side of town.

Her son wants to use the money to go into business. He has
never had a break and never had a job. Now he has a friend
who has a "deal." He begs for the money, and although his
mother refuses to give it to him at first, she knows that she must
eventually give in. How can she deny her son's pleading for his
first chance to do something for the family?

Soon the family learns that the son's "friend" has taken the
money and skipped town. Humiliated, the son confesses it's true.
His sister wastes no time tearing into him. Pouring out her con-
tempt, she screams at him for having lost for them all the only
route out of the hell in which they have lived for years. When
the sister finishes her tirade, the mother speaks:

"I thought I taught you to love him."

"Love him?" the sister demands. "There is nothing left to love."

Then the mother replies, "There is always something left to
love. And if you ain't learned that, you ain't learned anything.
Have you cried for that boy today? I don't mean for yourself
and for the family 'cause we lost the money. I mean for him;
what he's been through, and what it has done to him. Child,
when do you think is the time to love somebody the most; when
they have done good and made things easy for everybody? Well,
then you're not through learning—because that ain't the time at
all. It's when he's at his lowest and can't believe in himself 'cause
the world has whipped him so. When you start measuring somebody, measure him right, child, measure him right."

And that is a word that God speaks to the church through
Jesus Christ. For through Christ, and only through Christ, God
gives us the lens through which we must measure the worthi-
ness of people to receive our embrace.

Oh, I know how hard that is to do. We are such different
people. So many things threaten to divide us. And in many cases
they are very important things—matters of conscientious principle or righteous conviction. And in every matter there is bound
to be a difference of opinion. As the mountaineer said of his

pancakes, "No matter how thin I mix 'em, they always come out with two sides." So there are two sides to every issue. And what may look like an opinion to me may seem to you a commanding religious conviction. The Scribes and Pharisees were so sure they were right. They had scripture on their side. They could quote chapter and verse. Surely Christ's death on the cross represented to them the victory of right over wrong, the triumph of divine truth over heresy. Jesus was killed by people who had the scriptures down cold, but who knew not the spirit.

And if it was a tragic and blasphemous sin then, when people—in the name of righteous conviction—broke the body of Christ, is it any less a sin today when people, in the name of their own righteous conviction, sunder the body of Christ?

I may never agree with you about many things. But the genius of the Christian Church (Disciples of Christ) from its very beginning has been our magnificent obsession to allow our common commitment to the preeminent Christ to be the sole focalizing agency.

Need I remind you of our history? We are fond of saying that Thomas Campbell was a minister of the Presbyterian Church. Well, that's a classic understatement. He was, to be specific, a minister of the Old-Light, Anti-Burgher Seceder Presbyterian Church—a fragment of a section of a portion of a sect of the Church of Jesus Christ. And each of those adjectives represented a bitter division in the church that had been achieved through the legalistic *whereases* and stubborn *therefore be it resolveds* of some solemn church assemblies, that had made the tragic error of thinking the church belonged to them!

And when Thomas Campbell came to America, he was crushed to discover that those same political divisions—which had made little enough sense in Ireland and Scotland (where the political realities had produced the divisions)—had been imported with the church to America, where those political technicalities made no sense at all.

Not long after Campbell's arrival in America, he was asked to visit a few scattered Anti-Burgher Presbyterians at a community named Cannamaugh and to hold a "sacramental" celebration among them. Campbell was concerned for the many persons in other branches of the Presbyterian family who had not received the Lord's supper for some time and who were in attendance at this service. He proposed that all persons present were free to partake of the elements when they were offered, regardless of their presbyterial connection. And it was this glorious heresy, this magnificent sacrilege that ended Thomas Campbell's career as a Presbyterian and gave birth to the noble notion upon which the Christian Church (Disciples of Christ) was built: that reverent obedience to Christ is quite enough to make sisters and brothers of people and to make them all equally welcome at the family table.

Hence we came into being as a religious movement with this cry upon our lips, "No creed but Christ!" It was not a cowardly surrender to the lowest common denominator, but an expression of the magnificent obsession that impoverishes all other considerations.

In the ancient history of the Middle East, Cyrus was an important king. He appears in scripture, by the way, in the book of Isaiah. There is a beautiful—and reportedly true—story about Cyrus and a rebel chieftain named Caligula (no relation to the later Roman Caesar of the same name). This Caligula had some land on the southern border of Cyrus' kingdom. Cyrus defeated Caligula in battle and, complying with the rules of war at that time, Caligula and his wife were summoned before King Cyrus to receive the death sentence. Ordinarily the sentence would have been automatic. But Cyrus was impressed by this man Caligula as he stood strong and tall and courageous before him. So King Cyrus began to question him: "Caligula, what would you do if I spared your life?" Caligula replied, "Sir, I would return to my home with gratitude and remain for the rest of my life your obedient servant." Then Cyrus said, "And what would you do if I spared your wife?" And Caligula answered, "Oh, your majesty, if you would do that, I would gladly die for you."

So impressed was Cyrus that he required of Caligula only that he give an oath of allegiance to the king. Then he sent him home, a free man.

A short time later, when they were at home, Caligula and his wife were talking. He said to her, "Did you notice the beautiful marble in the king's palace?" She answered, "I didn't see it." "Then," he asked her, "did you see the magnificent tapestries on the walls of the palace?" "No," she replied, "I didn't see them." He said, "Then surely you noticed that Cyrus was sitting on a throne of gold." She said, "I didn't notice." "Well," he asked, "what did you see the day we stood before the king?" And she replied, "I saw only the face of one who said he would die for me."

One by one they all fall away—the marble, the tapestries, the gold, the things that tempt us, the grudges they smolder in us, the hurts we nurse, the opinions that divide us—they all fall away when we look upon the face of the one who died for us. Oh, beloved, we should be standing together on the mountaintop of divine grace, our hearts and voices united in a hallelujah chorus of praise to our Christ, instead of feuding in the foothills of our pet peeves and petulant prejudices.

Recently I spent a little time in the beautiful French Canadian city of Quebec. What a beautiful place and how steeped in history! It is the oldest continuously existing city in North America and our continent's only walled city. The people are justly proud of their heritage, which makes them what they are. And the official motto of the Province of Quebec reminds them of that. It's on the license plate of every vehicle on the street. You see it everywhere. It says, in French, *"Je Me Souviens"* ("I remember"). What they are, you see, is what they remember. Their memory has forged their identity.

And so with us Christians. It is our holy memory of the one who instructed us to be the church, "in remembrance of me," that makes us what we are. And it is in remembrance of him that we embrace one another, loving others as he loved us, accepting them as he accepted us. It is not what we are, but what he is, that makes it possible for us to embrace as Christian sisters and brothers all those whom he loves, however different they may be from us.

Is it necessary, is it absolutely essential that we must choose up sides and draw battle lines over every issue that comes along? Perhaps it is time for us recall how the apostle Paul achieved a working consensus among the Christians at Corinth—surely as diverse and disputatious a collection of Christians as existed! He said, "For I decided to know nothing among you except Jesus Christ, and him crucified" (1 Cor. 2:2).

"In remembrance of him," my brothers and sisters, we must embrace one another.